WHY CHARACTER?

The Personal Quest That Matters

WHY CHARACTER?

The Personal Quest That Matters

Vicente "Tex" S. Hernandez

Polaris Publishing

Manila, 2025

© 2025 Vicente Javier Stabile Hernandez
All rights reserved.

No part of this publication may be reproduced, duplicated, or transmitted in any form—electronic or printed—without prior written permission from the author. Recording of this work is strictly prohibited.

Image Credits.

Unless otherwise indicated, the images in this book were created using AI-assisted rendering tools, guided by the author's conceptual and compositional direction. These visuals serve as symbolic companions to the text, reflecting its philosophical and emotional themes.

This title—alongside blog articles on related topics and upcoming additions to the series—can be found at echoepolaris.com, echoesofpolaris.com, or by searching on Google Play Books or Amazon Kindle.

Distributed by Amazon Kindle.

Strive not to be successful, but rather to be of value.

Albert Einstein

CONTENT

CONTENT vii
Introduction 1
Chapter One: Can We Change? 5
    Why Change? 7
    The Three-point Strategy 10
Chapter Two: Character 15
    A Modern Scenario 18
    The Five Pillars of Character 21
Chapter Three: Intellectual Character 25
    Critical Thinking 26
    The Socratic Method 28
    A Heart for the Truth 31
Chapter Four: Ethical or Moral Character 35
    Believe it or Not 38
    Finding Answers 40
    Rights and Wrongs 42
    Getting Involved 44
Chapter Five: Performance Character 47
    Life is an Adventure 48
    Qualities Influencing Performance 53
    Loyalty Isn't Outdated 55

  The Optimistic Mindset............................ 57
  Your Next Move 60
Chapter Six: Emotional Literacy 61
  Personality Profiles................................. 63
  Emotional Extremes................................. 66
  In Conformity with What We Are 69
  The Controversial Psychotic Disorders...... 72
Chapter Seven: Social and Civic Character................. 75
  Social Intelligence vs. Skills...................... 76
  Alarming Statistics.................................. 77
  Acquiring Social Abilities 79
    Awareness 80
    Empathy... 81
    Bearing 82
    Authenticity 84
    Clarity.. 86
  Models of Communication 86
    The Linear Communication Models.... 88
    Other Models of Communication 89
  Key Lessons from This Chapter 91
Chapter Eight: Crises....................................... 93
  Life Challenges 94
  Developmental Crises 97
    Adolescent or Coming-of-Age Crisis ... 98
    Quarter-Life Crisis.............................. 99
    Mid-Life Crisis.................................. 100
    Late-Life Crisis................................. 102

    Do We Benefit from Crises? 102

    Depression 104

        Symptoms 105
        Physiological Foundations 106
        The Burnout Syndrome 107
    Life Lessons and Takeaways 108

Conclusion 111

About the Author 115

Other Works by the Author 117

Notes 119

Introduction

Those of us who wear glasses need an upgrade occasionally. This time, in a last visit to the optical shop I subscribe to, one of the new attendances by the name of Jane brought me around the endless display of frames and helped me to select one advising me on price and style.

I could not find the exact replica of my old pair, and I complained about it. 'New styles do not duplicate the old ones,' she said, 'Because fashion and taste change.' Wow! The conversation was turning philosophical... 'Could the latest fashion outshine the old?' I asked. She smiled and replied, 'It is your preference.' A smart answer. I initiated the conversation, but she followed it by changing the focus. In our country, curiosity about the marital status of any foreigner-looking individual is expressed in the following rhetoric question: 'Does your family stay here with you in the country?'

What followed was my own personal inquiry and curiosity about her. It turned out that she was from a city far away from the capital where I used to work. I asked her if she was married, and she simply said that she had a child. 'What happened to the father?' I asked and she answered, 'I abandoned him.' 'But, why?' I added with concern. 'Because he was lazy.' This was turning into counseling, and I decided to stop my probing by concentrating on the pair of glasses I had in my hands — which were not as nice as the ones I wear, which I believe makes me look younger; don't we always favor vain choices?

Jane was an exceptional saleswoman. She convinced me that 'The latest choice was just perfect to match the width of my face and provide a contrast to its softness.' Well, I had never thought of my face as soft, but at that very moment, I would have asked her to work for me if I had been in sales.

Being a skilled professional and, surely, a loving mother —along our conversation, I sensed the love she had for her child— does not guarantee a happy future, especially if Jane had issues with her boyfriend. Situations like this, much like many challenges we face in life, often require mending. But where do we start?

No one is free from the responsibility of his or her choices. No one has an easy life. It is a fallacy to think that we can avoid every responsibility and leave risk, frustration, or pain behind. Life is complicated.

The rich, the beautiful, the powerful, the smart, the lucky—and even the crooks—often show a type of pleasurable, worry-free lifestyle that we envy. We envy the golden cage, not realizing it's still a cage.

We see them in luxury yachts or cars, wearing designer clothes, spending money extravagantly, and enjoying fabulous vacations; we especially admire their looks on social media. But behind their thin layer of glow, we find sleepless nights, strained relationships, addictions, a fear of losing wealth, or the pressure to maintain an image. This is a weight difficult to carry, often a facade of an unsettling life.

Real-life stories are depicted in books like 'The Price of Privilege' by Madeline Levine, who uncovers the emotional toll of wealth on families, and documentaries like 'The Social Dilemma,' which expose the regrets of tech billionaires. The documentary 'Miss Americana' shows that the brightest lights bring only stress and pressure among stage artists.

The illusion of a perfect, worry-free life profoundly impacts society, especially the youth. Through the show of glamorous, wealthy lives people develop unrealistic hopes and goals. Unattainable standards bring about feelings of inadequacy and frustration.

A society that idealizes success, wealth, and status above all else fosters shallow values and relationships. The growing number of mental health issues, and even suicide, shows that there is something deeply wrong in the center of our modern, structured society.

Anxiety, depression, low self-esteem, identity loss, and social divides have become increasingly typical in modern society.

Our ability to respond to challenges often depends on our upbringing, background, values, and life experiences. We all know of people who despite tough circumstances learn the skills, land a decent job, step up, and improve their family's situation. The secret to true success lies in growing our physical, mental, and spiritual qualities in a balanced and harmonious way, embracing the changes it entails.

Chapter One: Can We Change?

We could say that personal growth depends on a desire to change. Each desire paves the way for what lies ahead, acting as the foundation, shaped by our capacity but not limited to it.

When it comes to abilities, strengths, and weaknesses, it is difficult to make an honest-to-goodness self-evaluation. Even though it sounds difficult and embarrassing —for some even unthinkable— we need some help here. Would you dare to ask others what they think of you? Would you dare to ask your partner, your boyfriend or girlfriend, your best friend, your immediate family, or a spiritual adviser? If married, surely your spouse would eagerly hurry to offer help. Would you accept whatever he or she tells you?

This is the measure of our true self. Nonetheless, because we generally have a better opinion of ourselves, even solicited advice goes usually to waste. This is expressed in the terms of the well-know, often quoted, old proverb 'The best business in the world would be to buy a man for what he's worth and sell him for what he thinks he's worth.'

People resist change because they're afraid to face the truth—it often bruises the ego. Other contributing factors include laziness, lack of motivation, and even lack of courage. The effort to change is frequently hindered by statements like, 'I am happy the way I am,' 'Why should I change?' or 'I don't care about change.'

Fig. 1: First generation, most popular mobile phones of the '90s.

Many may not even remember the innovative Nokia mobile phones of the 1990s, so popular that no competitor could challenge their sales. Everyone had one. Their Symbian operating system was unmatched. This began to change in the late 1990s and the first decade of the new millennium. The initial challenges came from Palm OS, Windows CE, and BlackBerry OS, followed by Apple's iOS in 2007. Google's Android in 2008 brought them all to their knees. Nokia's failure to recognize the need for change has been the focus of many studies; the fact is that Nokia was blind to what was truly happening and couldn't care less.

For starters, Nokia phones were being left behind by innovative technologies like the touchscreen. To top it all, Nokia's internal architecture was outdated and could not keep up with the demands of a multitasking environment. But the main reasons of their collapse were a type of corporate pride and defective partnership agreements. Nokia was so confident about the control that they had of the market that they failed to recognize the potential of the smartphone. With the sudden drop of sales, they thought only of a partnership with a company, Microsoft, that at that time was still scrambling to adjust to the new technologies. Nokia was too proud to deal or partner with the competition.

Would the story of any of us resemble Nokia's case study? Proud attitudes are the reason behind many of the trials that we experience in life. Outright mistakes, shortcomings, defects of character, and the full gamut of our deficiencies are difficult to acknowledge without humility and a desire to improve. The path of a loser is marked by pride and stagnation.

Why Change?

Why are we so afraid of rectifying our ways? Why do we put so much emphasis on what others might think of us? Our predecessors are often remembered for their contributions and legacies rather than their eccentricities. Would their stubborn denial of a mistake hold true even after they've left us? Not by any chance. They are history and their trouble irrelevant—unless they changed history. Their irrelevance extends to billions of people who have gone before us—of whom we know nothing. Why should we defend a mistaken opinion out of pride when sooner or later it will no longer matter? When you need to apologize—since both parties are usually at fault—do it without worrying about others' opinions. Haven't you noticed that ridiculous statements, stubborn opinions, or static roles—even when we're right—often bring laughter and pity from those around us? Think it over and hold onto this thought.

However, the answer to the question 'Why should I change?' is not just about what others see in us. The deepest reason to embrace change is because it is personal: "If you're not growing, you're dying." [1] Restlessness, conflicting desires, guilty feelings, misdirection, and many other types of insecurities make us all wish for a better version of ourselves. That better version of oneself is achieved through personal growth. In general, putting aside any psychological type of introspection, we need to start by the obvious which can be grouped into four areas of improvement: attitudes, habits, behavior, and the mastery of oneself.

Attitudes are stances; attitudes are passive. They reveal our disposition.

Habits, on the other hand, are essential. They are what keep us grounded and allow us to perform effectively. Without them, we often feel shapeless. We rely on habits to strengthen our resolve and harness the energy needed to accomplish what we set out to do.

Fig. 2: Can we change? Break the cycle.

Behavior refers to the way we act; behavior is active.

Mastery entails the ability to control our unrestrained passions and the obsessions we may develop over time, whether due to stress or medical conditions.

Lastly, we need to focus on a third question that will help solidify everything we've discussed so far: 'What should I do to change?' Making changes in the four areas mentioned above is most effective when you take it one small, deliberate step at a time.

The Three-point Strategy

We are all familiar with the rules regulating basketball games. Basketball originated in 1891 in Springfield, Massachusetts, USA, and was invented by James Naismith, a Canadian physical education instructor. He simply wanted to keep his students active indoors during the cold winter months.

Fig. 3: The three-point line.

The first game was played on December 21, 1891, at the International YMCA Training School in Springfield. Since then, the rules have evolved to improve the game.

One of the most significant innovations, the 'three-point line' or 'three-point shot,' was formally adopted by the American Basketball Association (ABA) in 1967. This rule has revolutionized basketball strategy.

The three-point strategy could serve as our model for staging change—if, like basketball players, we learn to use it effectively. At first, it might seem odd or even amusing. However, it is simply a way of focusing on concrete objectives.

The three-point strategy addresses a recipient or goal, followed by three practical objectives for improvement. To let the strategy speak for itself, see the following scheme, organized by the most common areas of concern, illustrating a simple methodology that anyone can use to stage progress.

- Improving the relationship with my spouse: (1) go out on dates, (2) offer voluntary help, (3) show affection through physical contact (i.e., holding hands).

- Getting closer to my children: (1) avoid overcorrecting, (2) pay them more attention, and (3) show affection in a physical way (i.e., kissing or embracing them when you arrive home).

- Dealing with my in-laws: (1) avoid quarreling, (2) agree on terms, and (3) use their resources.

- At work: (1) try to smile, (2) care for personal order (i.e., leave everything as it was before you came in), (3) be always proactive.

- Reaching out to my friends: (1) keep contact, (2) pay attention to their moods, and (3) offer your help when you can.

- Dealing with the not so friendly neighbors: (2) make it a point to greet them when you cross ways, (3) be of service, and (3) show interest for their concerns.

We could continue expanding our list to include various groups—for instance, homeowners, professional associations, alumni, employees, the company's board, salespeople, or vendors. Additionally, we could explore personal strategies and even focus on specific individuals with whom we aim to improve our relationships.

Obviously, the chances of success with this method depend on self-knowledge, which includes a clearer understanding of our limitations. We may have been doing things poorly for years without realizing what was happening around us. We might have even caused serious problems in our families or at work, blaming others for issues that actually stemmed from our own negligence, uncontrolled passions, vices, and the full spectrum of our personal flaws. We often believed that, simply because we had them, others had to accept our shortcomings.

To open our eyes, we need to understand what character truly is. The following chapters will offer insights that few other publications provide, giving you a new, comprehensive, and clearer understanding of the pillars of character. Eventually, you'll need to develop your own blueprint and revisit the 'three-point strategy' as a way of solidifying your resolve.

Freedom gives us the capacity to grow and become more effective. While no one can claim absolute freedom—after all, what kind of freedom would mean being free from sleep, food, traffic laws, social and family obligations, or respect for others?—freedom from personal defects is essential if we want to improve our character and unlock our potential.

Chapter Two: Character

We often admire people for their success, intelligence, or talent. But have you ever stopped to think about what really makes a person stand out? We're not talking about fakes, movie stars on a red carpet, or sports athletes after a championship. We interact with many people, and among those we deal with most often, we can identify qualities that make some stand out as different, yet still average. How is this possible? If they are average, what makes them special? We see in them a number of admirable qualities—some we even envy, simply because we don't have them. Can we develop those ourselves?

Humans are the only species in the planet that take fourteen to eighteen years to mature physically and psychologically. This seems to be a weakness if we compare ourselves to different species of the animal world. We seem to have reached a very low level of adaptation compared to the strength of the lions, the flight of the eagles, the skin of the crocodiles, and the impossibly numerous physical abilities of so many animals in the complex habitats existing in our world. Yet in our weakness, our reasoning capacity becomes our strength. Thanks to reason, we compensate for these physical inabilities and become stronger, fly to higher altitudes, and protect ourselves from the environment in infinitely better ways than any animal we know of. And so, we need more time to turn into a fully grown, mature individual.

Fig. 4: What separates us from each other?

Nonetheless, maturity is always a project, something we need to grow into. Maturity is a lifetime challenge, more than just a physical state. There is a strong connection between maturity, which is physical and psychological, and the development of what we call our character. Both involve processes of growth, self-awareness, and integration. Overall, we refer to this integrated process as the process of growing.

We talk about personal growth and character development, but we also need to see how they are integrated into our personality. Among the varied interpretations and descriptions of what personality is, we choose to define it as the range of distinctive qualities and traits of an individual, what makes us truly different from each other. Character on the other hand is the energy within that brings us to develop our potential. Personality highlights the traits that make us unique, while character drives us to focus on personal growth.

We all know that character matters, but let's be honest, how often do we give it the importance it deserves? It's one of those things, like good health or honesty, that we assume is important, though we rarely sit down to define it. What does character really mean for each one of us, and why should we care?

Character involves a process of transformation which cannot be set aside because what we end up becoming is critical. This process is as natural as moving from childhood to adolescence, becoming adults, and crowning our lives with the wisdom that comes with aging. We develop character throughout our lifetime, but like an old car, it is always in need of repair. How so?

Defects of character are always obvious. Many think that deficiencies define what we are—more than positive traits—and cannot be altered. Give credit to the ancient Greek philosophers who thought just the opposite. All of them—Stoics, Epicureans, Platonists, Cynics, Aristotelians, Hedonists, Pythagoreans, and Skeptics—viewed character development as a process of becoming or transformation; each philosophical school had a program. Stoics relied on virtue for transformation. Epicureans focused on the pursuit of a tranquil life to free themselves from unnecessary desires. Platonists emphasized education and ethics. Cynics rejected social norms and material desires to live according to nature. Skeptics sought transformation through the suspension of judgment. Pythagoreans found peace in mathematics, order, discipline, and purity. Hedonists capitalized on pleasure, whether by discipline or indulgence. Aristotelians proclaimed a gradual transformation of character built through habitual good actions. Aristotle nailed it: his ideas laid the foundation for modern personal development.

A Modern Scenario

The following paragraphs take a more academic turn—a necessary step as we lay the groundwork for the model introduced in this book. While the tone may shift, the aim remains the same: to make sense of the forces that shape us.

We have come a long way. Still, every philosophical model from the past has, in a way, been integrated into a multitude of present-day ideologies that uphold them.

We are familiar with the hedonistic and narcissistic ideas spread through the media, the skeptical attitudes of many public figures, and every government's pressure on policies in favor of a respect for nature—the Greeks called them Cynics. But, in the end, what makes

Aristotle's ideas so relevant as to dominate the modern character and personal development theories?

Over the centuries, philosophers and thinkers have come to understand that Aristotle's concepts of virtue and autonomy—and the way we acquire them through practice and the development of habits—as well as his theory of well-being, have proven to match our human nature.

Fig. 5: Aristotle of Stagira
(Wikimedia Commons, GPL License)

Anyone working on a meaningful theory of character eventually had to turn to Aristotelian ideas. Two of the modern pioneers, Carl Rogers (1961) and Abraham Maslow (1968), were among the first to develop what is called the *positive theory* about human nature. They agreed with Aristotle on the fact that people have the ability to grow and improve, and that humans naturally strive for personal development and psychological well-being as part of their inherent potential.

Rogers and Maslow have been followed by many. The internet is full of advice on personal growth. A natural wave of thought has eventually turned to define four key areas that set character development apart: the social, emotional, spiritual, and physical. However, the pioneers Jean Piaget (1896–1980) and Erik Erikson (1902–1994) who are given the credit for the development of the PIES model—that stands for Physical, Intellectual, Emotional, and social stages of human development—never conceptualized it. Apparently, a separate group of educators and psychologists coined it. "Nurturing the whole person—physically, intellectually, emotionally, and socially—is the key to unlocking one's full potential and leading a fulfilling life. This holistic approach to personal development, known as the PIES framework, has gained significant traction in recent years as educators, psychologists, and self-improvement enthusiasts recognize the interconnected nature of human growth."[2]

Piaget is best known for his theory of cognitive development (1920s through the 1950s) while Erikson's theory addresses the emotional and social aspects of development (throughout the 1950s and 1960s). Who could then claim the authorship of the PIES integrated theory 'unlocking one's full potential'?

The Five Pillars of Character

Only later in our historical journey, the *five integrated areas* changed into pillars. Is this a significant step? Pillars are friendlier than areas. Pillars can take a very defined and limited shape. Areas feel amorphous, vague. Together, pillars can support something greater—heavier?—than themselves.

Michael Josephson and a group of educators began discussions about six pillars of character in 1992. Josephson in his Institute of Ethics promotes trustworthiness, respect, responsibility, fairness, caring, and citizenship as "core ethical values that transcend cultural, religious, and socioeconomic differences."[3] Most recently in 2015, Curtis Florence reduced the number of pillars to five: integrity, respect, responsibility, fairness, and caring [4] to focus on personal development and individual character traits.

However, both Florence and Josephson speak more about developing core values than pillars. While they use the metaphor of "pillars" to symbolize the importance of each value as a key component of good character, their emphasis falls short of completeness. Character is not limited to the development of a few values, no matter how important an essential they might be. Josephson's six pillars are meant to serve as principles that help individuals shape their behavior, decisions, and interactions. Florence on the other hand highlights the role of his essential values as flexible, evolving guidelines that help individuals build their moral and ethical framework.

However, character is more than cultivating a set of specific habits. Character formation is a continuous and dynamic process that involves the development and integration of core values consolidated into pillars in a way like the areas proposed by the original PIES model. We are talking about values—a variety of them—grouping and shaping into separate pillars, and pillars interacting with each other to become the foundation of character development.

No other educator has been able to develop this concept better than Carlos Beltramo and his team. As a student, I can attest the impression that the presentation of his five pillars of character brought up among us; I could say that I was finally starting to understand and put loose endings together. Starting with its simplicity, his five pillars comprise the most basic needs of character formation—which follows a long scholarly tradition.

Developed as an independent theory, within the framework of human sexuality, the five pillars are but an alternative to sexual education programs. Their conceptualization offers a gleam of what could one day be one of the most convincing general models for character formation.

"Character is not, therefore, a univocal concept but a broad, multifaceted one. It can be said that character can be understood from different complementary points of view... Putting these aspects together in a complementary way, it can be said that they are like five pillars that support and define character education as a whole."⁵

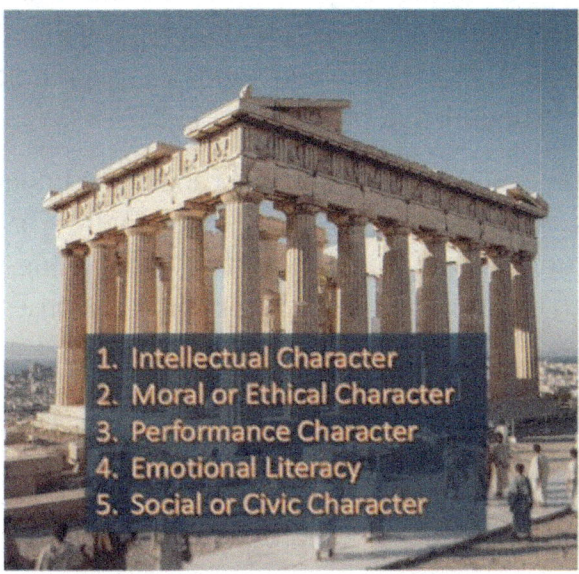

Fig. 6: The Five Pillars of Character
(Conceptualized by Carlos Beltramo)

In general, these five pillars could be described as follows:

(1) Intellectual Character: the habitual attitude of searching for knowledge and understanding as the foundation of our standard cognitive abilities, coupled with the cultivation of traits that guide reflective thinking.

(2) Moral or Ethical Character: the ability to understand how every action leads to its consequences,

shaped by internal values and principles that encourage thoughtful and responsible behavior.

(3) Performance Character: a permanent disposition to draw strength, ability, and motivation from any favorable or adverse circumstance, grounded in perseverance, self-discipline, and a commitment to benefiting oneself and others.

(4) Emotional Literacy: the capacity to understand, express, and establish an emotionally balanced connection between oneself and the world, alongside the ability to recover and manage emotional responses.

(5) Social or Civic Character: the integration of cognitive and emotional components to engage meaningfully and responsibly with others, fostering contributions to the well-being of a broader community beyond interpersonal and introspective dimensions.

The academic explanation of the five pillars of character highlights how they are interconnected. Since we are all interested in how they develop and how to apply them in practice, this presentation includes a carefully selected range of opinions and recommendations.

While drawing inspiration from Carlos Beltramo's conceptualization, the following framework includes an independent reflection on each pillar as a distinct entity.

Chapter Three: Intellectual Character

'Intellectual growth should commence at birth and cease only at death' (Albert Einstein).

When we first hear about intellectual character, we tend to think of it as something to do with special, extraordinary capacities—like being a genius or something only a few people have. But it's different. Intellectual character isn't about having a special skill; it's more about how we think, reason, and approach learning. It's a quality that anyone can work on and improve.

Being curious and wanting to learn are key to building this kind of ability. When you start to really crave knowledge, it pushes you to ask questions, look at things from new angles, and connect more deeply with the world around you.

These days, with so many choices and problems to solve, knowledge matters more than ever. That's where intellectual character comes in—it helps us think things through, see issues from different sides, and make better decisions. And the way we think shapes how we talk to others and handle relationships.

There's a lot to gain from developing intellectual character. Out of all the key traits that make up good character, this one might be the most important for growing as a person. It helps us face our flaws, admit when we're wrong, understand others better, and build stronger connections.

In emotionally charged conversations or heated debates, we often respect people who stay calm, admit what they don't know, and are open to hearing different views. Those are signs of intellectual character too—and the kind of qualities people tend to admire and trust.

Fig. 7: Shaping how we think.

Critical Thinking

In a time where it's easy to fall for fake news or strong opinions, having this mindset—being curious, thinking critically, and open to changing your mind—

really helps us figure out what's true and what's not. The rise of fake news all over social media and other platforms really shows why we need to develop more thoughtful, reflective ways of thinking. In a world full of misinformation, it's getting harder to tell what's real and what's not.

Misinformation isn't new, but it's becoming a bigger problem. With today's tech and how easily we can share things, it's simple for people to twist facts, edit images, and spread false stories that look real.

People with strong intellectual character won't just take shocking or suspicious news at face value. Instead, they'll pause, ask questions, check other sources, or wait for more info before deciding what to believe.

While intellectual character includes many virtues, critical thinking acts as its foundation. We could say that critical thinking is the core value of intellectual character because it upholds the way we approach knowledge, reason through problems, and seek truth. Critical thinking is the ability to analyze information, evaluate arguments, and make reasoned judgments. This skill develops gradually in those with a genuine curiosity to learn and a willingness to assimilate new concepts.

A key aspect of critical thinking is asking questions and developing the habit of consulting reliable sources. Today, the internet offers access to a vast array of standard, acclaimed, and specialized dictionaries, encyclopedias, search engines, and innovative digital tools—including artificial intelligence—capable of satisfying any intellectual interest.

The Socratic Method

Intellectual development has been championed by many philosophers and educators, with Socrates standing out for his logical approach and the profound simplicity of his method. Socrates emphasized the importance of questioning and seeking the underlying reasons behind beliefs and actions. His method, called the *Socratic Method*, is popular and involves asking probing questions to stimulate critical thinking.

The key features of the Socratic Method are based on a form of cooperative dialogue.[6]

1. *Questioning and Dialogue* – The process begins with systematic questioning, encouraging participants to examine and articulate their values, principles, and beliefs. By critically analyzing facts and convictions, the dialogue focuses on the reasons that justify any position.

2. *Elenchus (Refutation and Testing)* – A central feature of the Socratic Method. This step involves probing the motivations and assumptions of participants. Through rigorous questioning, contradictions and inconsistencies in their arguments are exposed, prompting deeper reflection.

3. *Dialectical Debate* – Participants improve their views through an organized exchange of ideas. A thesis is presented and then critically examined through

challenges and counterarguments, fostering a more profound understanding of the topic.

Fig. 8: Ancient roots, modern talk.

Instead of group discussion, you can question yourself about any relevant issues of your concern and strive to find the answers you are looking for. Whether alone or in a group, the aim is to train ourselves in critical thinking through analysis and logic, eventually leading to sound conclusions. Ultimately, critical thinking seeks truth, coherence, and deeper understanding rather than blind acceptance or passive agreement.

Let's get down to a practical exercise. Today, during a meal at home, ask your family about the reasons for keeping pets in the house. 'Why pets? Why would anyone keep pets at home?' Just give a lame excuse to introduce the topic and add, 'Even though they don't eat you for breakfast, some pets have been proven to be disloyal and turn against their masters.[1] You can prepare ahead and talk about Brenda Guerrero and her bulldog or any other case you've come across in your readings. What happened to Brenda? The bulldog, named Scarface, went after her in the couple's Tampa home on New Year's Day in 2017. When her husband, Ismael, stepped in to help her, the dog turned on him. The couple's 22-year-old son tried to intervene but failed to stop the dog. The three eventually managed to escape, leaving the dog outside.

Follow the Socratic method. You will be surprised to see how lively the conversation turns! And if not, you can follow up with your own reasoning and conclusions to spark the dialogue by asking for their opinion.

You can use the same strategy to repeatedly bring up topics you've read about or that your family is interested in. The newspaper has an endless capacity to spark conversations on any topic imaginable. In doing so, you are introducing an interesting method of training. You have become a capable moderator, equipped to address interruptions, disrespectful or arrogant attitudes, and closed-minded views. By doing this, you are helping your family develop intellectual character.

This exercise can be done at home or in any other environment you frequent. It can benefit friends, students, colleagues, and subordinates. You can even practice it casually with people while waiting for a doctor's consultation or during an overseas professional trip.

Questioning is not necessarily an act of mistrust or defiance toward authority—it depends on our tone, intentions, and genuine desire to uncover the truth. However, questioning should not be used merely as an intellectual exercise to sharpen the mind. Its true purpose is to seek clarity and wisdom.

A Heart for the Truth

A heart committed to the truth seeks accuracy, honesty, and understanding rather than convenience, personal gain, or comfort. In this, the role of our intellectual character is critical. We have come to understand intellectual character as a deeply ingrained quality, an internal drive to seek and comprehend the true foundation of our own knowledge, which enables us to act with integrity. This is about a genuine desire to know the truth, culminating in an honest acceptance of the most fitting outcome.

However, to be objective about the truth—avoiding subjective interpretations that lead nowhere—we must structure our process of verification.

The entire effort begins with a sincere attitude of openness. Second, we question assumptions—often presented to us as facts—and consider alternative interpretations. Third, we verify the information we possess, or that we can find, against the assumptions we've identified. To do this, we use whatever tools we have at our disposal or consult people who can provide objective answers. Fourth, we evaluate our options which, lastly, will enable us to judge honesty on any matter under scrutiny and choose only what in our opinion conforms to the truth.

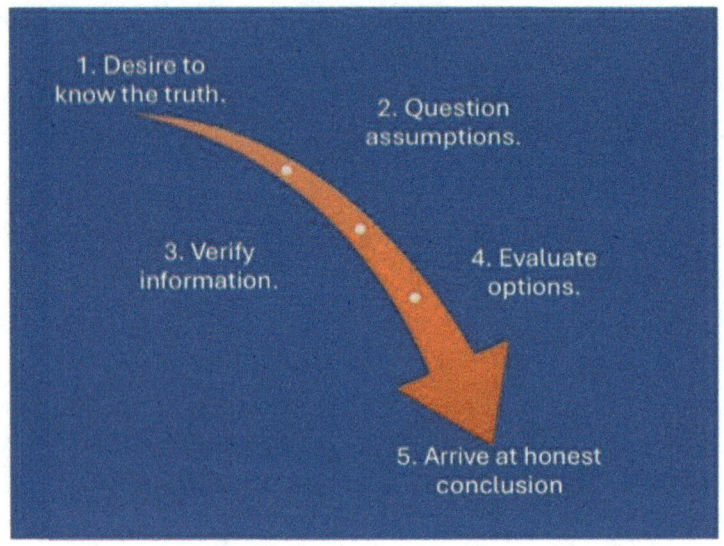

Fig. 9: The Intellectual Character Drive.

It is becoming increasingly common to hear news about the deaths of actors, public figures, and even dignitaries—news that often turns out to be false. The individuals behind these hoaxes are typically motivated by a desire to attract viewers or *likes*, which are often monetized by social media platforms. It is also common to encounter—on platforms like Facebook, for instance—AI- or digitally-generated images of monsters, astonishing discoveries, fossilized giants found in remote mountains, new civilizations, supposed evidence of extraterrestrial life, and other imagined phenomena. Although obviously fake, these posts still deceive many into believing they are real.

We also receive, daily, a growing number of text messages, emails, and even audio calls promising amazing rewards, incredible returns from deposits in certain banks, and job offers with salaries usually reserved for top executives. These are often mixed with the constant stream of advertising we receive from major companies in the country, in every form imaginable. This flood of communication is largely the result of our personal information being sold—or obtained through piracy by unscrupulous individuals who infiltrate our electronic networks to gain an advantage and, ultimately, profit.

We could go on describing the manipulation of the media by powerful lobbying groups who, though a minority, dictate the opinions of the majority; or by political groups and ideologies that distort the news to ridicule and discredit facts, attacking anyone who opposes their views or contradicts their agendas. This is a mad world. More than ever, we need to develop our intellectual character, and the method we have just described can be of great help due to its simplicity and thoroughness.

All of this is part of the critical thinking process. Critical thinking finds its true significance when it is driven not merely by a thirst for truth, but by a deep-rooted sincerity of heart. Without these—truth and sincerity—

critical thinking becomes a hollow exercise; one might win a debate yet ultimately deceive oneself in the process.

Sincerity is the habit of communicating and acting in accordance to the way we feel, the beliefs that we profess, the thoughts that we nurture, and the desires that we raise in a genuine, honest, and respectful manner.[7] A sincere person carries with it an aura of authenticity and integrity which is attractive and compelling. Being honest with yourself and others is essential for a fulfilling life. However, it requires the effort to recognize personal truths and the willingness to share them with those who deserve your trust.

Sincerity, love for the truth, integrity, openness, and honesty all form part of what we call the first pillar of character: intellectual character. These are qualities that hoaxers, swindlers, scammers, deceivers, and impostors will likely never understand. Even less, would they recognize the connection between intellectual character and the next foundational pillar: moral or ethical character. Those who profit from deception are unlikely to acknowledge the existence of a moral compass, let alone allow it to guide their actions.

A sincere search for the truth demands a strong moral and ethical foundation, which reinforces the unity of the five pillars of character. Much like the harmonious melody of a well-composed piece of music, these pillars work together, creating a balanced and meaningful approach to life.

Chapter Four: Ethical or Moral Character

Paul Johnson—British journalist, popular historian, speechwriter and author—once said that if people affirm universal physical laws as certain—like Newton's laws of motion, the laws of universal gravitation, thermodynamics, electromagnetism, etc.—why is it so difficult to accept that there are also universal ethical laws? It's surprising, but there are several ethical principles that most people agree on, and we can even break them down into these twelve categories [8]:

The Golden Rule. *Treat others as you wish to be treated.* This principle, found in many religious and philosophical traditions, emphasizes empathy and reciprocity. It encourages us to treat others with kindness, fairness, and respect, just as we would want to be treated.

The Principle of Non-Maleficence. *Do no harm.* This ethical guideline emphasizes avoiding causing harm to others, either through actions or omissions. It is a foundational principle in fields like medicine and law but is also broadly accepted in everyday life.

Justice and Fairness. *Equality and impartiality.* Most people agree that individuals should be treated fairly, and that resources and opportunities should be distributed justly. This includes equal treatment under the law, fairness in decision-making, and opposing discrimination or bias.

The Right to Life and Safety. The belief that every person has the fundamental right to live and be free from physical harm or threat is widely accepted across cultures. This includes both the right to personal security and the duty to protect others from violence.

Honesty and Truthfulness. Lying and deceit are generally considered unethical in most societies, especially when it undermines trust and harms relationships. While cultural norms may vary, honesty is typically regarded as an essential value for healthy interactions.

The Principle of Reciprocity. Give and take. This principle reflects the idea of mutual benefit and cooperation. It suggests that we should help others when we can, expecting no immediate return but fostering positive social bonds in the long term.

Respect for Autonomy. People generally agree that individuals have the right to make their own choices and decisions, especially regarding their own bodies and lives, as long as these choices don't harm others. This principle underpins the concept of human dignity and personal freedom.

The Principle of Beneficence. *Do good.* Beyond merely avoiding harm, this principle emphasizes the active pursuit of actions that contribute to the well-being of others, such as helping people in need or improving society.

Respect for Property Rights. The right to own property and not have it stolen or destroyed is widely accepted across cultures. This principle involves respect for others' possessions and the social rules governing ownership and theft.

The Principle of Compassion. Many cultures and religious traditions promote compassion, which encourages caring for others and showing empathy, especially toward those who are suffering or in need.

Accountability and Responsibility. A common ethical belief is that individuals should be held accountable for their actions and take responsibility for the consequences of those actions, whether good or bad. This principle is important for maintaining social order and trust.

Respect for Truth and Knowledge. The pursuit of truth and knowledge, while understanding its limits, is generally valued in most societies. It is considered unethical to intentionally spread misinformation or suppress knowledge for selfish gain.

Far from being an exhaustive list of ethical laws, we find in the outline above a pattern of behavior, a basic moral compass, which encourages responsible decision-making and develops resilience against unethical practices.

Believe it or Not

You might remember it. *Ripley's Believe It or Not!* began as a newspaper panel series in 1918, created by Robert Ripley. From there, it expanded into books, radio shows, television programs, museums, and more, all showcasing oddities, curiosities, and unusual facts. First published in *The New York Globe* as *Champs and Chumps*, it later evolved into a radio show (1930s), a television series (starting in 1949), books, and museum exhibits before officially adopting the title *Believe It or Not!*.

Fig. 10: Martin Laurello could rotate his head 180 degrees (*Believe it or not*, 1940; Wikimedia Commons, GPL License)

The TV series had several successful versions, with notable hosts like Jack Palance in the 1980s and Dean Cain in the 2000s. Audiences were captivated by strange-but-true stories, extraordinary human feats, natural wonders, and mysterious phenomena—from bizarre cultural traditions to rare animal species and unexplained events

The primary goal of *Believe It or Not!* was to entertain, educate, and spark curiosity by presenting remarkable, surprising, and sometimes unbelievable facts and stories from around the world. It aimed to challenge perceptions of reality and encourage viewers to marvel at the diversity and mystery of human and natural phenomena. The program's tagline *Believe It or Not!* reflects its invitation for audiences to question their presentations and decide for themselves whether the extraordinary stories were credible.[9]

What do we believe in? Everyone believes in something beyond the sensorial level. There is a reality beyond what we can see and touch that we must acknowledge. We know there are other continents on Earth even if we've never stepped outside our city. We accept someone as our father or mother without asking for a birth certificate or a DNA test. Most of our beliefs are founded on the trust we place in information received from external sources—including the people and the channels we find more reliable and appropriate.

What, then, is the ethical and moral foundation of your beliefs?

Finding Answers

I am not going to answer this question, because you should be the one to find the right answers. I can only say that if ethical and moral values exist, there must also be an ethical and moral foundation. This requires reflection and a sincere desire to reach an honest level of certainty.

Fig. 11: A quiet moment with life's deepest question.

The reality outside the scope of our eyes is called belief. Every person is bound to have some kind of belief. We are guided by what we believe in, but if our belief is groundless, we become disoriented. What, at some point in time, was meaningful has turned to dust, disappeared, and dropped us into an apparently bottomless pit.

Everyone, at some point in life, asks himself or herself questions like: 'Why am I here?' 'What is the meaning of life?' 'What happens after death?' We all need a moral compass that aligns with established ethical values. Without this moral compass, life hardly makes sense.

People without a moral compass can easily run amok when pressure builds up and they are unable to remain in control. We increasingly hear about the growing number of individuals involved in spree killings, which are becoming a security nightmare during large gatherings. In a broader sense, we can also include other forms of amoral behavior, which often seem rooted in the absence of an ethical foundation.

For instance, regarding homicides, the United Nations Office on Drugs and Crime (UNODC) reports approximately 450,000 intentional killings per year. The latest UNICEF report states that 370 million girls and women worldwide have experienced rape or sexual assault before the age of 18—equivalent to approximately 1 in 8 females. Additionally, 650 million individuals (including both girls and boys) have experienced some form of sexual violence in childhood, encompassing both contact and non-contact incidents.

Without a moral or ethical compass, there is no obvious basis for altruism of any kind, moral anarchy takes over and the rule of the self prevails. We have no duties or obligations except to ourselves, and we need to weigh no other considerations except our own interests and pleasures. [10] But if, on the other hand, we discover the true meaning and purpose of a moral and ethical life, we find fulfillment in living for others and for our communities—building a truly human society and contributing to the happiness and well-being not only of others but of ourselves as well.

Ethical and moral character is developed not only through observation, education, service, and intentional practice, but also through convictions that are deeply rooted in our human nature—convictions we must reflect on and uncover. It is further shaped by a deliberate desire to find foundational values in our lives. We develop ethical and moral character through reflection and meditation on the purpose and meaning of life, and by questioning what we find unethical within ourselves—something that often requires time away and a peaceful environment inviting reflection.

Rights and Wrongs

Ethics helps us discover what is good to follow it and what is bad to avoid it. Moral or ethical character enables us to make morally sound decisions and act ethically in life. Ethical behavior focuses on understanding and following ethical values. If our ethical values are poor, our decisions might lead us to waste not only our talents but even our opportunities.

There is a fascinating study involving the *toss-a-fair-coin* paradigm, which examines honesty and cheating behaviors. "We asked each child to toss a fair coin in private and to record the outcome (white or black) in a paper sheet. We rewarded only who reported white. We found a fraction of reported whites significantly larger than 50%, uniformly across age groups. This suggests that some children cheat when cheating is profitable, and they are not observed.

In a second treatment we told children not to cheat. This reminder reduced the probability of reporting white by 18% on average, and significantly more in girls.[11] Research using this method has demonstrated that, like adults, children sometimes cheat when they believe they won't get caught. However, as the test above illustrates, the extent of cheating can vary depending on factors such as age, moral development, and the perceived fairness of the situation.

On the other end, Felix Warneken, a researcher at the University of Michigan, who has spent years studying toddlers and their behaviors, suggested that children display altruistic tendencies from a very young age.[12] For instance, toddlers often help others spontaneously, without being asked, rewarded, or observed by their parents. This challenges the notion that we are inherently selfish.

How do we develop this sense of morality—the internal mechanism that helps us distinguish right from wrong? From a young age, we learn to behave and live according to certain moral values taught by our family and the environment we engage in.

While these external influences shape an individual's moral framework, we also acquire ethical values through personal experience and internal reflection.

Fig. 12: Finding strength in ethical foundation.

Getting Involved

Through experience, we learn to evaluate right and wrong by observing the impact of others' actions—including our own—and how people react to them. Internally, we all sense a natural inclination to support the ethical principles outlined earlier in this section. We got the basis; we're hardwired for it. It's built into who we are.

One of the best approaches to developing inner ethical or moral character is by getting involved. Life offers a tremendous variety of opportunities to collaborate on projects for the welfare of others. Simple actions, like considering the well-being of those who work for us, our colleagues, friends, and even superiors, can transform our perspective. We will immediately notice misunderstandings and confusion regarding essential attitudes that require clarification. Whether or not we are in a position to act, our personal effort to identify and rectify erroneous principles is the starting point of change.

However, if ethical and moral values are natural to us, how can we explain their absence in those who challenge or even oppose them? This absence can be attributed to a variety of external and internal factors.

External influences, such as one's environment—exposure to violence, for instance—and cultural backgrounds, can significantly shape ethical behavior. Internally, factors like early life experiences, family dynamics, education, mental health challenges, personality disorders, or trauma play a crucial role in shaping ethical values.

These factors may hinder an individual's ability to act ethically. Despite that, everyone, no matter how wrong or confused his or her stance is, retains the capacity to act with freedom in favor of some basic ethical principles or contrary to them.

This underscores the importance of teaching and learning. Philosophers and religious traditions assert that moral and ethical character is developed and refined through education and intentional practice. Learning guides us to act in accordance with universal moral principles, rather than selfish attitudes and interests.

Fig. 13: Giving isn't just charity—it's a force that restores dignity.

The true essence of moral behavior lies in this question: 'Can we genuinely act for the sake of others, without personal gain influencing our actions?'

Moral character is developed through learning and a sense of what is right, nurtured by the personal effort to live and work for the benefit of others. This is where the relevance of acquiring meaning truly resides.

Chapter Five: Performance Character

When it comes to expectations, Gretchen Rubin—the *New York Times* bestselling author of *The Four Tendencies*—seems to outshine academic management experts. Her personal research offers a somehow unique perspective, classifying people based on what she calls *outer* and *inner* responses.

Can the way we respond to expectations really say something meaningful about who we are? Maybe yes, maybe not. But if we think of these responses as rooted in natural tendencies or capacities, then perhaps the answer is yes. Still, can we draw a clear connection between expectations and capacities?

Rubin's study is based on online questionnaires completed by volunteers eager to participate. She makes a key distinction between expectations others place on us and the ones we place on ourselves. *Outer expectations* typically involve things like work demands, family responsibilities, or other external obligations. *Inner expectations*, on the other hand, are personal—like, as she puts it, keeping a New Year's resolution.

She then combines these two types of responses to form four distinct personality types. "Upholders respond readily to both outer expectations and inner expectations.

Questioners question all expectations; they meet an expectation only if they believe it's justified, so in effect they respond only to inner expectations. Obligers respond readily to outer expectations but struggle to meet inner expectations. Rebels resist all expectations, outer and inner alike."

The big question is, are we limited by our inner capacities? In other words, can we perform better, overcome a limitation? We are now coming face to face with the concept of *value* or, classically, *virtue*. If we understand that developing a habit—the actual definition of what a virtue is—can change the way we perform, yes, we can say that we can become better people, better performers. Forging strong values is like improving our personal skills and strengths, as both play a key role in shaping our character.

'Upholders,' 'questioners,' 'obligers,' and 'rebels' all respond and grow in virtue through challenges. We need challenges to forge strong values, and challenges are found only in a life of adventure.

Life is an Adventure

We refer to migration studies as the interdisciplinary field that draws from several academic disciplines, primarily anthropology, genetics, linguistics, archaeology, paleontology, history, and human geography. Though not all their findings are conclusive, they show that migration challenges have always been—and still are—a vital part of the human spirit and the drive for adventure.

Studies show that the Indo-European migrations led to the spread of language families like Latin, Greek, Germanic, Slavic, and Celtic across Europe. The Bantu migration from West-Central Africa to Eastern and Southern Africa reshaped much of sub-Saharan Africa. Pressure from the Huns and the collapse of the Roman Empire triggered the movement of Germanic and Slavic tribes into Europe, laying new foundations.

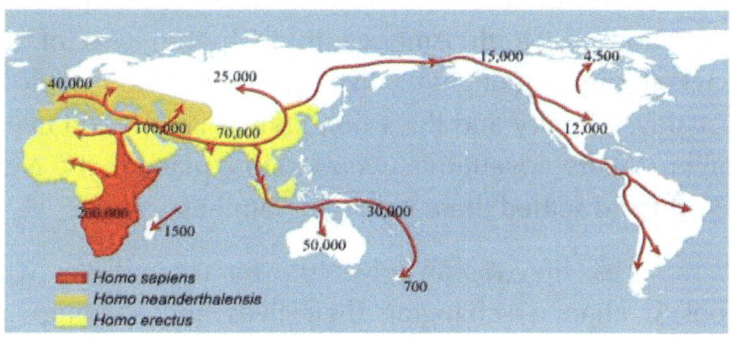

Fig. 14: Early human migrations
(Wikimedia Commons, GPL License)

We also know of the Athabaskan migration in North America, the rise of the Aztec and Inca empires, the development of the Indus Valley culture, and the Austroasiatic migrations. One wave of migration followed another—like the Viking expansions and the Mongol conquests—which pushed into and settled new territories in Europe and Asia. Europeans later followed, populating many of these lands, especially in North and South America, South Africa, and Australia.

Few migrations have been captured with the depth and clarity of the European westward expansion in North America, as told by Louis L'Amour. Drawing on witness accounts, historical records, and oral tradition, his storytelling brought the frontier to life—and earned him the honor of being the first writer to be awarded the Congressional Gold Medal.

His 89 novels and dozens of short stories depict the history of 17th- to 19th-century European mass migration to North America through the lives of the Sackett saga, gunfighters like Kilkenny and Hopalong Cassidy, Chantry and the Talon families, Flint, and many other solitary adventurers who found a place in the New World and settled there with their families.

Yes, life was an adventure for the millions who took a chance—changing their lives and shaping our future. Whether through voluntary migration or the pressures of war, hunger, and hardship, migrants have always needed toughness, resilience, and determination.

Today, life is still an adventure. For those migrating in search of better opportunities and higher wages. For newlyweds starting a family in a borrowed home on a modest income. For recent graduates working long hours to build a future. For family men juggling two or three jobs to support their loved ones.

Life is an adventure—and we should keep it that way. A new challenge should always be on the horizon. That's how we cultivate the values that define performance character.

We don't just face adventure—we seek it. That's why we chose to walk 100 kilometers along the Portuguese Way to Santiago de Compostela. We only needed a plan and a budget that fits your needs—thanks to the wide variety of *albergues* (pilgrims' hostels) in every town, this journey is accessible to many.

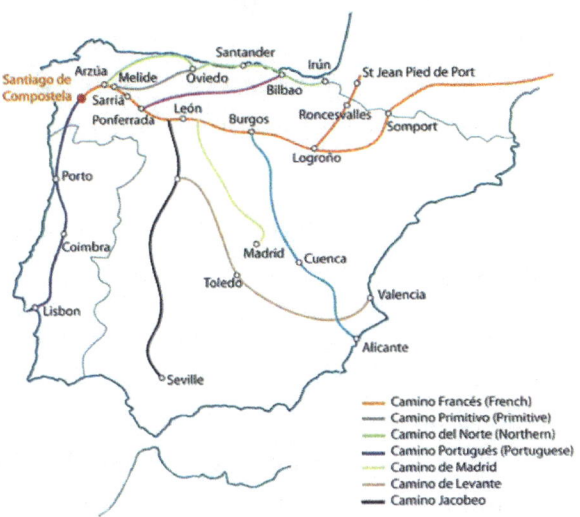

Source: https://hiketheway.com/camino-routes
Fig. 15: The traditional routes of the Camino de Santiago.

Some might ask, "Why walk when you can drive?" That question fades quickly once you're on the trail, surrounded by strangers who become companions, each with their own reason for choosing the long road. We met dozens of pilgrims who, despite pain and fatigue, saw The Way as an adventure worth living.

On the day we arrived, 2,600 people completed the pilgrimage. From our own experience—and from the people we met along the way—we learned three essential values: commitment, determination, and resilience.

- Commitment — without it, you'll never begin.

Every stage is set by the number of kilometers you must walk each day. That structure demands planning, discipline, and a decision to show up—day after day. It's a commitment to your plan. Rain or shine, we crossed paths with the same people each morning. Their consistency built friendships, momentum, and a rhythm that carried us all forward.

- Determination — the will to persevere once the journey begins.

One afternoon, we met a Canadian woman in her sixties who had developed painful blisters by the third day. We helped arrange a taxi to bring her to town and get patched up. The next morning, we saw her again—slower, but smiling. She told us, "I didn't come this far to stop now." Determination is what keeps you walking when comfort says stop.

- Resilience — the ability to endure and adapt when faced with real adversity.

Many pilgrims walk despite physical limitations that would discourage even the most daring. Hans, a retired 82-year-old German with a prosthetic leg, was one such person. We passed him day after day—and found him, on the final day, enjoying a beer in Santiago.

Adventure builds character. And character, in turn, makes the adventure worthwhile.

The adventure lies in the plans we make—for ourselves and our families—in the way we manage our projects, and in the dreams we keep alive. (For those interested in exploring this idea further, I've written about it in 'What Are My Chances? Life Management Explained.')

Worthy objectives and clear steps bring with them challenges that shape us and strengthen our character along the way.

Finding adventure in life lifts our spirits and gives us reasons to keep moving forward. Whether it's out of necessity, as a sport, or just a weekend with the family, every adventure offers a chance to grow in this aspect of character we call 'performance.' Seeking adventure is a sign of a youthful spirit—one we should nurture and develop throughout our lives.

However, to find adventure in both the ordinary and the extraordinary, we need to go deeper—understanding the roots that lead to performance and examining the qualities we must cultivate. Each of these qualities can become a personal project, if we're willing to recognize its importance and choose to develop it. That choice—to grow deliberately—is itself a kind of adventure, one that begins within.

The Eight Qualities Influencing Performance

Performance Character traits are connected to self-control and self-management, shaped by the development of specific habits, which we will briefly outline as *perseverance, diligence, courage, resilience, optimism, initiative, attention to detail,* and *loyalty*. Studies indicate that these virtues or habits significantly influence performance in both personal and professional settings.

Fig. 16: We move forward through habit, passion, and purpose.

These eight qualities reflect a type of character that stands out in any organization. We admire them in friends or colleagues whose values drive them to commit to long-term goals. They demonstrate thoroughness and reliability in every task they take on, effectively overcoming obstacles, confronting risks and fears, recovering from setbacks, and maintaining an optimistic outlook. Their proactive and loyal attitude stretches beyond the company they work for, embracing family and friends as well.

We truly admire these qualities in others, but they can also be ours if we set ourselves to work on them and make them our leitmotiv.

While all eight performance character habits or virtues are essential, it's reasonable to argue that loyalty and optimism are valued above all. Without them, every other aspect of performance character becomes harder to attain. Persevering in a task—showing diligence, courage, and resilience—is very difficult without the underlying values of loyalty and optimism.

Loyalty Isn't Outdated

Sports events—whether official competitions, friendly games, or just practice—always end with winners, losers, and sometimes quitters. Regardless of the outcome, one value stands out in sports: loyalty. Quitters—those who give up or walk away from what they committed to—are often looked down on and forgotten.

Loyalty matters not just in sports but in any task or commitment we take on. Loyal people are more likely to stick with their goals, work hard, show courage, and bounce back from setbacks. Loyalty is a clear sign of real commitment. It is a "practical disposition to persist in an intrinsically valued (though not necessarily valuable) associational attachment."[13]

Loyalty doesn't seem to matter as much today as it once did. Take Gen Z's job-hopping habits, for example. Because they're more digitally aware and have different ideas about what work should look like, younger generations can sometimes be a challenge for employers.

Compared to earlier generations—Millennials who value collaboration, Gen X who are independent, and Boomers known for their strong work ethic—today's culture often seems less consistent. And this isn't just about the workplace. It shows up in relationships and friendships too, where commitment and trust don't always hold up. Even amid success, this shift can leave people feeling empty or disconnected.

Still, loyalty isn't outdated. It can fit right into today's fast-paced world—especially when combined with integrity. Even if someone only stays in a role for a short time, sticking to the terms of an agreement, doing their best, and keeping an open attitude toward dialogue with employers shows both loyalty and character. It's not about how many jobs we've had, but how we show up in each one. People who are reliable, honest, and open are always in demand.

Quitting only makes sense when we're giving up something harmful to us. Anything that goes against our ethical or moral values should be set aside. However, even what seems harmful deserves careful evaluation. For example, staying loyal to a friend or close relative—even when they turn against us—can reflect both maturity and strength of character.

Loyalty is strengthened by optimism. Like light in a photograph, optimism brings out the colors and depth in the printout of our life.

The Optimistic Mindset

The invention of the incandescent bulb stands as a significant and inspiring story. From Humphry Davy in 1802 to Thomas Edison in 1879, success and failure shaped numerous variants until Edison ultimately perfected it, giving us what we enjoy today. Edison famously said, "I have not failed. I've just found 10,000 ways that won't work." Many of life's failures are people who did not realize how close they were to success when they gave up. Without his perseverance and optimism, Edison would have failed—though nobody would truly believe that without his invention today we would still be using candles or oil lamps.

Chinese history is rich with incredibly intricate works of art and craftsmanship that reflect deep perseverance, patience, and extraordinary attention to detail. Some of the most famous examples span across dynasties and artistic forms—from jade carving to silk embroidery to porcelain.

Take, for example, the Imperial Chinese porcelain of the Ming and Qing Dynasties. These pieces display incredible detail in blue-and-white or multi-color designs, often depicting dragons, flowers, or historical scenes. The artistry and technical mastery demonstrate unmatched precision.

Fig. 17: Mastery is forged in dedication.

Add to this the photo-realistic Suzhou silk embroidery, the intricate wooden puzzle balls—spheres carved from a single piece of ivory or wood—and, out of the Han Dynasty, the funeral suits made of thousands of jade tiles sewn together with gold or silver wire. Together, they offer a powerful measure of the detail and dedication that only the reward of creating a beautiful piece of art can bring to the artist.

None of this work would be possible without an optimistic and positive vision of the outcome.

Why is optimism so remarkable? Because it drives us toward success, no matter how difficult or complex the task becomes.

A clear understanding of what we want—or need—to achieve, combined with a love for detail and a genuinely optimistic outlook, should be part of our daily lives.

Attention to detail isn't limited to major inventions, works of art, or impressive achievements. It's also found in sticking to schedules, pushing through fatigue, and facing the many small challenges life throws at us. Nothing in our lives should be wasted. Still, none of it holds meaning without a positive view of what we do and why we do it.

We need reasons. Sometimes even the simplest reason is enough—but we can grow beyond that. Like the craftsmen who built the cathedrals of the past, we might come to see that we're not just earning a salary or supporting a family but building something greater. We're offering a valuable service—no matter how small—or contributing to the well-being of others and the success of the organization we work for.

Optimistic people often inspire those around them, recover more easily from setbacks, and find better ways to solve problems. On the other hand, pessimism usually leads to discouragement and failure. Some argue that optimism isn't realistic, but this view often reflects a negative mindset.

Even when it seems unfounded, optimism can lift our spirits—especially when it's combined with other good habits like persistence and effort.

Your Next Move

I like to insist on the fact that life is an adventure. Life works better when you treat it that way. If that feels out of reach, start with a challenge—something that gets you moving.

Challenges don't have to be risky or dramatic—they just need to stretch you. You will be surprised at how much sense you can gain in life through challenges. The best way to pursue them is through projects.

A project gives form to a challenge. It turns intention into action. Whether personal or professional, projects help you build habits, sharpen character, and connect your skills to the world around you. They fill your spare time with purpose—and often, with surprising results.

Pick a challenge. Make it a project. Then let it shape you.

Chapter Six: Emotional Literacy

One of the most important aspects of personal growth is knowing how to process one's own emotions and those of others. Reacting to an emotional response has often been regarded as a weakness of human nature. Greek philosopher like Plato, Aristotle, and the most representative thinkers among the Stoics considered emotions potentially dangerous. They saw emotions as 'irrational' and called them to restrain through subordination.

Extreme facts of our human nature expressed in, for example, running amok or committing a crime of passion have influenced cultural elements in the Asian, Western, African, and American traditions. Public displays of strong emotions have often divided commoners from the upper classes in England (the 'stiff upper lip' in the British tradition), brought about Confucian teachings on the suppression of any type of personal emotion, and encouraged the concept of "honne" (true feelings) and "tatemae" (public facade) in the Japanese culture.

Contrasting cultural extremes, we also find very positive elements like the search for harmony and balance in Asian cultures and by leaders among the Zulus and in native American tribes. Christianity has been a big contributor to values like love for God and neighbor, inner peace and serenity in the face of contradictions and setbacks in life. All these historical elements have fostered a better understanding of the emotions in the way they are generated and regulate our lives.

Fig. 18: Understanding and processing emotions.

Peter Salovey and John Mayer coined the term 'emotional intelligence' (EI) in 1990. They were preceded by Edward Thorndike in 1920 who introduce the idea of 'social intelligence'—or the ability to understand and manage people—and Howard Gardner in 1983 who proposed the theory of multiple intelligences and opened the way to EI. A few years later in 1995, Daniel Goleman popularized the term, making EI a complement of IQ (Intelligence Quotient[14]).

Emotions are profoundly shaping modern culture and influencing the thoughts, actions, and creativity of people around the world. Emotivism and personalism have divided certain sectors of society, shaping influential movements such as the Woke Culture. Regardless of the influence, a balanced study of emotions helps us understand how we acquire them and how they enhance our capacities.

You might know that most of the emotions we carry with us stem from our upbringing and childhood experiences. For instance, growing up in a household steeped in anger or disrespect can seep into our very self, becoming as natural to us as breathing. We acquire good and bad emotional responses from our upbringing. Without dwelling solely on the flaws inherited, we can also say that we have gained countless positive traits too.

Personality Profiles

Emotional literacy involves understanding how to process one's own emotions and those of others, but it is preceded by a greater awareness of our emotional makeup. Because emotional responses are intimately linked to personality profiles, we find in Alexandre Havard's primary temperaments the perfect fit to understand how our emotional responses relate to our biological makeup.[15] Alexandre Havard, the founder of the Virtuous Leadership System, distinguishes four personality types.

The Choleric. Decisive, goal-oriented, and ambitious, this temperament is marked by a quick temper and swift action, driven by passion and a strong sense of justice.

The Choleric personally calls for balance in its assertiveness, through humbler attitudes, and a greater focus. For the Choleric, cultivating prudence is essential.

The Sanguine. Optimistic, outgoing, and enthusiastic, the Sanguine is easily excited and emotionally expressive. They find joy and pleasure in communication and interaction with others.

Sanguine people need to counteract the tendency toward inconsistency, foster perseverance, and keep excesses under control.

The Melancholic. Being analytical, thoughtful, and idealistic, the Melancholic tends to be introspective but shows a deep emotional capacity and a strong sense of empathy.

The Melancholic needs to build greater self-confidence, overcome fears, become more assertive, and avoid inaction.

The Phlegmatic. Always calm and composed, the Phlegmatic shows confidence and a reluctance to display anger or excitement.

Being steady and even relax in the way of facing problems, the Phlegmatic might lack zeal and decisiveness and turn passive when action is needed.

Fig. 19: Take the Temperament Test →
https://temp.hvli.org/temp-intro
(Alexandre Havard © 2025 - Virtuous Leadership).

In his books *Virtuous Leadership* and *Created for Greatness*, Havard explains that most people are not "pure" types but a blend of two, with one being dominant and the other secondary. He refers to these as "secondary manifestations" or "composite temperaments."

It is even possible to combine not just two but three primary temperaments. A dominant temperament, when combined with the other primaries, results in twelve secondary forms. When these are further linked to a third temperament, they produce a spectrum of tertiary personality types—subtle nuances that shape one's behavior.

However, it is important to note that temperament identification is a tool for self-knowledge and growth, not a box that limits behavior. Our biological makeup is not deterministic; freedom and our capacity for change are among our greatest assets.

Discovering our temperament type greatly aids in understanding our emotional responses and in correcting the negative aspects of our personality. It offers us the opportunity to grow and become more balanced, well-rounded individuals.[16]

Emotional Extremes

Understanding our emotions—especially the extreme ones—can help us find ways to use the good and manage the bad. Normal ups and downs, whether too much or too little emotion, can usually be improved with the right approach. More serious issues, like bipolar disorder or anxiety disorders, need medical care and are beyond what we're focusing on here.

Hyper-emotional states involve things like mood swings, restlessness, talking a lot, high energy, impulsiveness, and strong emotional reactions. For some people, this is just how they are all the time; for others, it happens temporarily—often brought on by stress, tough situations, or intense experiences.

On the other end, emotional deficiency shows up in people who struggle to express or even recognize emotions. They might avoid emotional situations, seem distant or detached, rely only on logic, or prefer to be alone. They may show little facial expression or body language, lack empathy, or appear uninterested. This kind of emotional low energy can make it hard to connect with others or handle emotional situations well.

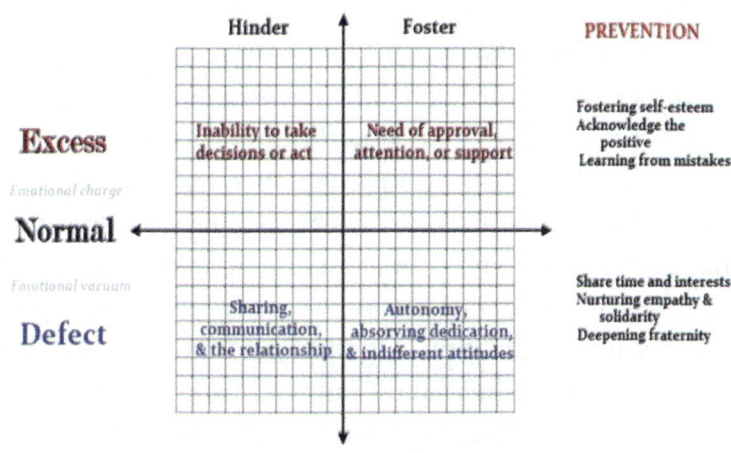

Fig. 20: The Emotional Chart.

We can manage emotional extremes in practical ways—even without clinical intervention. When emotions feel off or inappropriate, we can still regulate the feelings they provoke. Because we can turn our feelings around, we have the ability to work through them.

The first step is tolerance: staying calm and resisting the urge to react immediately. But tolerance isn't just about enduring discomfort. It also involves:

(1) Stepping back from the situation.

(2) Viewing it from multiple perspectives.

(3) Holding off on making quick judgments.

The award-winning documentary *The Rescue*, directed by Elizabeth Chai Vasarhelyi and Jimmy Chin, chronicles the incredible 2018 mission to save 12 boys and their coach who were trapped in a flooded cave in Thailand. It's a gripping story of courage and teamwork.

Towards the conclusion of the documentary, a volunteer, the British civilian cave diver Rick Stanton, recalled his feelings and how he managed them during the rescue. "We had no idea whether we were going to encounter dead bodies. We were stealing ourselves from that eventuality. I know what I was prepared to bump into because I'd visualized it very, very carefully. I'm a great believer in visualization. I try and put emotions in a box. I can visualize a shelf, and I put the box on the top shelf, and I leave it there, and I do what I need to do." A practical advice like this can make it easier to deal with emotional extremes.

Both children and adults can experience emotional imbalances, which often stem from underlying psychological patterns. *Excessive emotional reactions* are frequently driven by low self-confidence, a tendency to interpret situations negatively, and a fear of making mistakes.

On the other hand, *deficient emotional responses*—where emotions seem muted or absent—are typically marked by a lack of interest in developing communication skills, self-centered attitudes that disregard solidarity, and a tendency to view emotions solely through the lens of personal gain or profit.

Together, these patterns highlight how emotional extremes—whether excessive or deficient—can reflect deeper issues in self-knowledge and interpersonal relationship.

Working out every aspect related to hyper or defective emotional stages translates into a happier and more fulfilling life.

In Conformity with What We Are

We begin to understand the balance between emotions and facts when we consider who we are and what we're capable of.

As discussed earlier, emotions are part of our human nature—shaped by our biology, psychology, and personal history. But emotions alone shouldn't guide our decisions. Our abilities—like reason, empathy, self-awareness, and imagination—help us manage emotions and respond to reality more thoughtfully.

Emotions and reason aren't enemies. Emotions give meaning to facts, while reason keeps our emotional responses in check. Learning to balance both is key to developing what we've called throughout this chapter: emotional literacy.

The balance between emotional responses and reason has been greatly damaged in recent days by constructivist and postmodern theories. These theories are, in fact, harming younger generations by drowning their minds in a sea of uncertainty and relativism.

Social constructivism[17] suggests that our identity—including things like gender and race—is shaped by social influences, not just biology. Postmodernism goes a step further by questioning the idea of absolute or objective truth. These two ideas helped form queer theory, which argues that gender and sexuality are flexible, changeable, and based more on how we express ourselves than on biology.

As a result, today's culture often puts personal feelings and imagination at the center, treating them as the main sources of truth.

The documentary film *What Is a Woman?* produced by The *Daily Wire* in 2022 and featuring Matt Walsh as commentator, has sparked significant controversy.

Supporters of the film argue that the interviews and personal accounts effectively challenge modern definitions of womanhood promoted by transgender ideologies. Critics, however, point to the complexity of the issues and claim the film oversimplifies them. At the heart of the debate is the question, "What is a woman?"

The documentary defends a biological and traditional view—that a woman is an adult human female—rejecting the cultural confusion caused by current ideological trends.

Fig. 21: Questioning current modern ideologies.

Skepticism about gender fluidity, subjectivity, and relativism is presented through interviews with doctors, therapists, professors, and transgender individuals. The film also raises concerns about the increasing push for medical transitions in minors, including the use of puberty blockers, hormone treatments, and surgeries.

However, what scientific and psychological evidence supports the claims of constructivism, postmodernism, and queer theory? Which of these ideas are backed by facts, and which are not?

The Controversial Psychotic Disorders

Powerful lobbying groups—often supported by wealthy donors and tech companies promoting gender-focused agendas—are attempting to make truth relative. However, the version of "truth" they promote often contradicts well-established scientific and medical facts, which are being selectively ignored or dismissed.

In psychiatry, mental health conditions that involve a break from reality—such as delusions or detachment—are known as *psychotic disorders*. The ideological basis of some current cultural trends reflects similar patterns of disconnection. For example, schizophrenia—characterized by disorganized thinking and false beliefs—and schizo-affective disorder—which combines symptoms of psychosis with mood disturbances—are clinical examples of how severe detachment from reality can manifest.[18]

Dissociation is not limited to specific psychiatric diagnoses; it appears across a range of conditions and circumstances. Examples of this include brief psychotic episodes triggered by intense stress, which can cause temporary detachment from reality. Drug withdrawal or exposure to toxic substances may also lead to dissociation.

In mood disorders, particularly bipolar disorder with psychotic features, dissociation can occur during manic or depressive episodes. Severe depression is sometimes accompanied by psychosis, contributing to a break from reality. Neurocognitive disorders, such as dementia or delirium, often involve confusion, hallucinations, or delusions, further altering an individual's grasp on reality.[19]

Fig. 22: Disassociation from reality is a serious psychological disorder.

It is important to underscore the potential dangers that some emerging postmodern and constructivist theories may pose to our understanding of mental health. By questioning the foundations of psychological and psychiatric research, these perspectives risk normalizing dissociative disorders—conditions marked by disruptions in memory, identity, or perception—as mere variations of lived experience rather than serious clinical concerns.[20]

Consider this a warning to those who embrace constructivist and postmodern theories: dissociation from reality is a serious condition. Those who suffer from it eventually become impaired— unable to relate to others, emotionally unstable, and trapped in a psychosis where they believe they are isolated and constantly misunderstood for who they perceive themselves to be.

Chapter Seven: Social and Civic Character

Social and civil characters aim to improve our ability to live as active members of society. Life is more than just living together in a society where we're forced to accept others for practical reasons—like needing electricity, food services, and all the systems that keep society running.

Living in a community without real connection is still a form of isolation, and that kind of life can feel empty. Over time, it can even lead to mental health issues—consider the loneliness and challenges brought by the 2020-2022 pandemic. It's only when we connect with others that we begin to find real purpose and sense in life.

Studies on communication and isolation were initiated by Edward Thorndike early in the 20th century but his contribution on social intelligence became relevant only later after his death with the development of psychology and sociology.

Thorndike's idea of social intelligence emphasizes the combined role of intellectual and emotional abilities in engaging meaningfully with others. His concept went beyond basic social skills, offering a more comprehensive and holistic view of social communication. Thorndike defined social intelligence as "the ability to understand and manage men and women, boys and girls—to act wisely in human relations."[21]

In simple terms, it's the ability to relate well to others and respond appropriately in different social situations. [22] It involves understanding people and knowing how to interact with and respond to them effectively.

Thorndike's ideas gained broader recognition only in the late 1980s, with the rise of emotional intelligence.

Social Intelligence vs. Skills

The ability to thrive in social interactions goes beyond having a set of skills. Social skills are learned behaviors—things we can be trained to do. Social intelligence, however, is deeper. It integrates those skills into a person's natural way of being, making them feel instinctive or second nature, as if the person was born with them.

For instance, someone might take a course on communication and learn techniques like maintaining eye contact, asking open-ended questions, or using positive body language. However, if they don't internalize these habits—if the skills remain surface-level, under stress, at home, or when relaxed around close friends, they may quickly revert to old habits like interrupting, becoming defensive, or shutting down. In such cases, the learned skills haven't become part of the person's character. That's the difference: social intelligence makes the behavior consistent, not conditional.

Common social skills include active listening, empathy, conflict resolution, and teamwork. Social intelligence allows these abilities to sink in and shape one's personality over time. In this sense, social intelligence is the deeper capacity that enables people to absorb and apply a wide range of social skills naturally and reliably.

Alarming Statistics

It's easy to assume that social and civic character belong solely to public or professional life. But the truth is, our most basic social skills are first cultivated at home—long before they shape our communities.

Today, those home-based skills are in decline, as reflected in global marriage and divorce statistics. Over the past few decades, marriage rates have dropped sharply while divorce rates have climbed, though patterns vary widely across cultures, regions, and economies.

In the U.S., for example, the marriage rate fell from 16.4 per 1,000 people in 1946 to just 6.2 in 2022—the lowest ever recorded.[23] Roughly 43% of first marriages end in divorce. That number rises to 60% for second marriages and 73% for third. The average length of a marriage before divorce is eight years.[24]

'Marriage dissolution rates have become a critical indicator of social transformation across the globe. Understanding global divorce rates provides valuable insights into cultural shifts, economic pressures, and evolving relationship dynamics that define modern society.

Fig. 23: Communication bridges relational breakdowns.

The variation in divorce statistics worldwide is remarkable, ranging from India's exceptionally low 1% divorce rate to Portugal's staggering 94% rate, highlighting the profound influence of cultural, religious, legal, and socioeconomic factors on marital stability.' [25]

Reason behind these numbers are varied and confusing. Many believe that economic, cultural, religious, environmental, and social factors encourage separation.

However, few dare to name the deeper culprits: shaky commitments, fast-food romance, and the rise of consumer-style love—where intimacy is treated as a product, not a promise.

Even fewer recognize that many of these relational breakdowns could be addressed through basic interpersonal communication skills.

It's striking how often those who teach social strategies professionally struggle to apply them at home—where poor listening and unchecked ego quietly unravel what public performance cannot repair.

Beyond technical mastery, the challenge consists in internalizing social abilities as enduring traits of character.

Acquiring Social Abilities

Recent studies on social intelligence highlight five key areas that prepare us for effective social interaction.

The latest models emphasize (1) awareness, (2) empathy, (3) bearing, (4) authenticity, and (5) clarity.[26]

Awareness

Awareness is the ability to read people and situations in context, allowing us to choose the communication strategies that are most likely to lead to understanding and positive interaction. It means paying attention not just to what is said, but also to how it's said, what's not said, and the overall mood or dynamics of the situation. You will get nowhere unless you develop the habit of active listening and observing nonverbal cues.

Fig. 24: Essential social abilities (Freepik).

Take some time to reflect on a recent conversation with friends, coworkers, or family. For example, what did you learn from your last talk with a colleague? What did you notice that gave you a clue about how that person was feeling at the time?

This kind of awareness helps us respond wisely, avoid misunderstandings, and build stronger relationships.

Awareness also requires objectivity and the right attitude. Don't let emotional impulses cloud your judgment or show in how you express yourself. When people feel free to speak to you—without being interrupted, noticing your effort to understand their point of view—they'll naturally give you more insight into who they are.

Socially intelligent people are always tuned in to the situation and the needs of others. Awareness helps us respond thoughtfully and develop a sense of empathy as well.

Empathy

Empathy is the ability to connect with others and build a sincere bond and interest in one another. True empathy can't be faked. Pretending to care is usually obvious—even if you're a skilled actor. Since empathy is built on small, meaningful details, any lack of sincerity will eventually come to light.

The secret of empathy lies in discovering the richness of each person. Every individual we meet—every encounter we experience—can change us, especially when we see others as a gift. From this perspective, even the most challenging interactions can help us become more open, genuine, welcoming, and ultimately, happier.

No matter how different we feel from others, or how much their opinions differ—or even if they show an unfriendly attitude toward us—we can always respond with respect and understanding, opening the door to better communication. The key is to avoid making quick judgments about others.

As a fundamental principle, always remember that, despite our differences, the sincere expression of respect—shown through attention, eye contact, avoiding interruptions, and, when appropriate, sharing feelings or offering help—can create a meaningful bond between people.

Bearing
Bearing is the impression others have of us, reflected in the confidence we project and the way we communicate.

Some say that a facade comes with youth, especially during those difficult adolescent years when we're all searching for an identity. Others continue maintaining that facade well into adulthood—imitating the behavior of trendy celebrities or changing their appearance and mannerisms just to fit in. These are often seen as laughable behaviors that can lead to disrespect or ridicule.

Bearing encourages us to be authentic, but also to strive for improvement. We all have flaws in our character that need work. Awareness helps us read people and situations, but it also helps us notice how others respond to our quirks and personal style. In addition to reflecting on the impression we leave, we can ask for honest feedback from people we trust—relatives, friends, or colleagues—to help us identify and work on our flaws.

A good friend of mine, motivated by a desire to grow in his roles as a father and husband, asked his family to give him written feedback at the end of the year to help him form personal resolutions. That was a bold move. His daughters asked him to be more open and attentive; his wife wanted him to be more patient; and his son thought everything was fine. The experience turned out to be positive. His family gave him a kind of road-map, and in doing so, he came to understand how they truly felt.

Of course, feedback isn't always easy to accept. Another friend of mine, after receiving several consecutive negative evaluations at work, finally realized that something had to change. Like all of us, he needed to stay humble, give credit where it was due, and ask himself, 'Do their comments hold up?'

There's always room for improvement. We grow and mature by addressing the areas where we fall short. It helps to ask ourselves, 'What are the values I stand for? What do others see in me? Am I faking my image?'

Reflect on what you're good at—your strengths—and use them as a springboard for growth. Cultivate a sense of humor but be mindful not to hurt others with your comments. Humor can lighten conversations and help navigate difficult moments. Stay positive. Negative thinking and discouragement lead nowhere. Moods are manageable; they shift when a more positive and optimistic perspective is introduced.

Fig. 25: Feedback can bruise or build—how we receive it shapes who we become (*Freepik, Yanalya*).

Bearing involves developing habits such as expressing gratitude, learning to listen, pausing before speaking, apologizing when necessary, staying humble, and acknowledging mistakes. It also means staying calm and composed when others react negatively. Maintain mental and emotional balance. Along with good grooming and hygiene, maintain a personal yet respectful style of dress—even when you're alone or in a relaxed setting.

Authenticity

Authenticity can be described as the quality of being honest with oneself and with others. It is the opposite of being phony. Authenticity means communicating the truth, even when the truth is difficult or uncomfortable.

Lies are always damaging and lead to mistrust. They are often used as a form of self-protection, but the truth eventually comes to light and undermines our credibility. It's not worth it. When we cannot speak the truth, it is better to remain silent. This is especially important when it involves sharing personal information—our own or others'—which is usually protected by the right to privacy and the respect owed to a person's dignity and good name.

Often, people tend to simply echo popular opinions and may even cross the line of respect, slipping into gossip and backbiting. Many lack authenticity because they haven't developed their intellectual character—which, as defined earlier in this book, relates to how we reason and engage with knowledge. Popular opinions are rarely the result of personal reflection; they are often repeated so frequently that they start to feel true just by repetition. Without genuine dialogue and a diversity of perspectives, conversations become dull, uninspiring, and lacking in substance—in other words, a waste of time and unhelpful in building meaningful relationships.

In contrast, speaking from the heart and being honest about our true feelings—even acknowledging our flaws and mistakes—encourages sincerity and openness among others. But this kind of honesty also requires us to live by our core beliefs and values without compromise, to resist peer pressure, and to be willing to say no when necessary.

Clarity

Clarity is the ability to communicate in a straightforward manner, use language effectively, explain concepts well, and be persuasive. Clarity is the ability to express ideas in a simple and understandable way. We often assume that others understand what we say, but our explanations can sometimes fall short, missing the nuances in our own minds.

It's always valuable to pause and reflect on how we express ourselves, following conversational conventions to enhance communication: (1) know your audience and understand who you are speaking to; (2) be concise and specific, organizing your thoughts mentally and breaking down information—taking a moment to think before responding; (3) read widely, use a dictionary, and learn from others by observing how they appeal to emotions and use logical arguments.

No matter how much practice or experience we gain, there's always room for improvement in how we express ourselves. Given the importance of this, it's time to discuss models of communication.

Models of Communication

Not everything is as simple as it seems. After describing what social intelligence is and offering some guidance on how we can develop social abilities, it's important to introduce some basic—but essential—information about models of communication.

Social intelligence and communication models are deeply interconnected. "Models of communication simplify or represent the process of communication. Most communication models try to describe both verbal and non-verbal communication and often understand it as an exchange of messages."[27] Models offer a way to represent how meaning is exchanged within a social context.

Fig. 26: The complexity of modern communication.

Communication is essential in all organizations and relationships. By reflecting on how we've communicated in the past, we can better understand our mistakes and recognize the need to correct them.

Misunderstandings often occur—whether with friends, family, or coworkers—and the most common cause is misinterpreting what others mean.

Our experiences should prepare us for a better future by helping us improve the way we communicate.

The Linear Communication Models

The first group falls under what are called linear communication models. These are the simplest models and, as the name suggests, are directional—similar to one-way traffic signs we see throughout our cities.

These models distinguish between the **sender**, the **message**, the **channel**, and the **receiver**. The Shannon-Weaver model added an important additional element: **noise**.[28]

This first group is very straightforward in what it represents.

Examples include a professor delivering a lecture at a university, TV, YouTube, or radio advertisements promoting retail products, a salesperson giving a sales pitch, or a warehouse manager giving instructions to employees.

Effectiveness in these situations increases with the speaker's credibility, the use of the most appropriate communication channel, and the clarity of the message, which should be convincing for the intended audience.

Noise, understood as any external factor that disrupts communication, plays a critical role and can negatively impact the process.

For instance, if some employees are absent when the warehouse manager explains how to handle specific equipment, they may unintentionally damage it due to a lack of knowledge. Similarly, a professor might be unable to deliver a PowerPoint presentation if the projector malfunctions. In another case, noise from nearby construction during a sales pitch could distract the audience, causing them to lose focus and miss important information.

Other Models of Communication

All communication models beyond the simplest involve two or more directions. In basic conversations between two people, both take turns sending and receiving messages—this forms the basis of interactive and interpersonal communication.

When more people are involved, communication includes not just words but also non-verbal signals like posture and facial expressions. This reflects the transactional model, which emphasizes how communication builds both relationships and meaning at the same time.

You can see this in meetings, workshops, and even in online chat groups. Chat groups use digital tools—like emojis, GIFs, audio messages, join/leave alerts, delivery receipts, images, and videos—to add emotion, context, and instant feedback to their exchanges.

We view communication as an exciting process of learning. It draws us out of isolation and connects us with others. We learn from every exchange, no matter how trivial the cues may seem. Through communication, we gain insights not only about those we interact with but also about cultural and social trends—even ideological shifts.

Fig. 27: Understanding how chat groups work is key to social communication (*Freepik*).

Imagine a chat group where people swap opinions about their favorite restaurants. It's more than just food talk—it's a goldmine of insight. The way people agree, disagree, or follow strong voices in the group reveals a lot about how we connect and influence each other. In fact, many companies study these conversations to shape their products.

As group members, we don't always have to jump in. Just watching how people interact can teach us a lot about good communication. We also start to see who prefers what, what annoys them, and what makes them tick. In short, we learn how to understand others—and connect better because of it.

Key Lessons from This Chapter

Social intelligence—as the ability to understand social cues and manage relationships well—helps us handle complex social situations by finding better ways to respond.

Communication models—linear, interactive, or transactional—are simply interpretations of what we experience every day. However, having a basic understanding of how these models work is important for improving how we respond to these complex social interactions.

Social intelligence and communication models come together in the five key areas that support effective social interaction:

1. Awareness
2. Empathy
3. Bearing (demeanor)
4. Authenticity
5. Clarity

Through them, we build trust, show understanding, and deliver clearer messages—helping us recognize right from wrong in social situations. By focusing on these five areas, we make communication less confusing and more effective.

Chapter Eight: Crises

Crises are part of life. None of us can boast a record free of them. At various moments in our lives, we have felt the need to better understand what was happening within us. This chapter presents a description of the most common crises people experience—insights that can surely help anyone navigate the storm.

Ordinary days bring with them ordinary problems. These problems can accumulate and develop into situations that seem to spiral out of control. Such situations may escalate into crises when external factors—like financial instability, job-related uncertainties, or interpersonal conflicts—intervene. How we face these crises often depends on our character (shaped by the five pillars introduced earlier in this book), our current physical and mental condition, and the external support we can rely on.

However, it's often hard to meet these conditions—especially when dealing with things like negativity, loneliness, rejection, uncertainty, debt, betrayal, disloyalty, anxiety, discouragement, personal struggles, depression, or emotional burnout.

It would certainly be helpful to take a few practical insights from this book to build basic skills and avoid making life more complicated. We've learned that seeking more information about any matter of concern helps develop our intellectual character. In the same way, gaining a better understanding of what crises involve can help us navigate their complexities.

This guide is not meant to replace clinical or professional advice. Instead, it's designed to serve as a first-aid kit for the common situations people find themselves in.

Life Challenges

Rather than viewing these challenges through a pessimistic lens, we can see them as opportunities to discover life as an adventure. Challenges drive away boredom and make our lives more engaging. Everyday challenges also reveal that basic management principles—such as leadership, communication capacity building, problem-solving, financial management, and planning—are valuable tools we can benefit from. Understanding life management principles is just as important as overcoming personal weaknesses and striving to become a better person.

Often, the ordinary difficulties we face can be eased through better planning and clearer communication.

Management skills are often essential for handling the everyday difficulties people face. These include the pressure that comes with situations such as getting married, having a baby, applying for or starting a new job, moving to a new home, city, or country, paying bills, or managing conflicts.

However, the most challenging life events tend to involve more radical changes, such as losing a home, losing a job, going through a breakup, or facing serious health problems—whether due to an accident or medical complications that limit our abilities. These events can disrupt a person's sense of stability and lead to stress, anxiety, or emotional pain.

Fig. 28: Behind every task is a person juggling love, duty, and the pressure to provide.

Major changes or difficulties can trigger a crisis if a person's ability to cope is not strong enough. People with a history of trauma or unresolved emotional issues may struggle more when facing challenges—even those that seem minor. When environmental pressure combines with poor stress management, it can lead to irrational behavior (such as mood swings or unreasonable demands), anxiety, addiction (such as consumerism), or a shift in priorities—where self-centered attitudes take over and important values are sacrificed. In some cases, it may even lead someone to live a double life, with symptoms that border on dissociation or resemble features of schizophrenia.

The new realities brought about by radical changes often lead to circumstances that are likely to remain for some time—situations people must learn to live with. The most important stage in the healing process is *acceptance*, which we can transform into an optimistic attitude by turning away from negative thoughts and focusing on the positive. Acceptance requires, to a certain extent, *detachment* from what we appear to be losing and *hope* for what we might gain in the future. Being realistic means acknowledging that circumstances have changed.

Throughout this process, we need to deal with *worry*. Worry is deceptive—it makes us expect the worst and pulls us away from the best course of action in the moment. Worry leads to anxiety, which can become a dead end. We don't solve problems by worrying about them. We should avoid listening to those who only focus on the negative—including our own worries.

Professionals—psychiatrists, psychologists, educators, HR specialists, and counselors—agree that worry and anxiety are on the rise, both in frequency and intensity. There has been a sharp increase in anxiety-related diagnoses. More people report persistent worry, students are experiencing greater academic stress, workplace anxiety is a growing concern, and counselors address it in nearly every session, regardless of age or background.

Still, there are some home remedies we can rely on to handle what worries us. David A. Carbonell recommends working on:[29]

1. Acknowledgment. When we acknowledge that worry is a key factor, we give ourselves a chance. Worry manipulates both thoughts and emotions. Without giving in to it, we should accept that it can be managed and controlled.

2. Set aside worrisome thoughts and deal with them later, when the time is right. Learn to ignore your first instinct to react and focus instead on changing how you respond to worry.

3. Reduce worry's influence by developing a sense of humor. Don't take everything so seriously—most things have a humorous twist.

4. Set aside specific times to worry instead of doing it constantly. Carbonell refers to this as *worry appointments*, a technique that helps you regain control overanxious thoughts.

Developmental Crises

Crises related to life passages are often referred to as *transitional crises* or *developmental crises* which capture the idea of significant life changes or transitions.

We find among them the coming-of-age crisis or the transition to adulthood, the quarter-life crisis, typically experienced in the late 20s to early 30s, the mid-life crisis, and the late-life crisis, associated with aging or retirement.

Fig. 29: From youth to old age, each chapter asks something new of us (*Freepik*).

Adolescent or Coming-of-Age Crisis

Adolescence brings major emotional, physical, and hormonal changes as the brain rewires, and the body matures. Physical changes often include acne, hair growth, body odor, menstruation in girls, and broader shoulders or a larger Adam's apple in boys.

During adolescence, teens often go through strong emotions, mood swings, and questions about their identity. They start exploring their sexuality and may feel more vulnerable or self-conscious.

A mix of uncertainty, desire for independence, rebellion, social pressure, and peer influence can affect their behavior and relationships. If not managed well, these impulses can sometimes lead to serious issues like addiction or violence.

For adolescents, some of the greatest support comes when they open up to someone they trust—a positive role model who offers patience, understanding, and encouragement. Being able to share their physical and emotional changes is essential to making sense of them and learning to accept themselves.

This stage of life often brings emotional highs and outbursts. Self-control and balance can be supported by regular exercise, good sleep habits, a healthy lifestyle, and creative hobbies. For those with high energy or busy schedules, better time management can help reduce stress, anxiety, and even depression—which should be addressed early if noticed.[30]

All in all, adolescence can be a time of great personal growth. Young people often pursue ideals with enthusiasm, and when these are guided by positive values, they can build a stronger sense of self and purpose.

Quarter-Life Crisis
Many people in their mid-twenties to early thirties—sometimes even earlier—go through a period of uncertainty, anxiety, and self-doubt about their direction in life.

This often happens when starting adult life after finishing school, graduating from college, beginning a new job, or entering a relationship. Young adults may feel inadequate, unhappy with their careers, financially unstable, or unsure about their identity, goals, and future. It can be a very challenging time.[31]

Overcoming a quarter-life crisis starts with patience. Taking time to reflect on our values and future plans can help us find clarity and direction. It's a great moment to begin shaping our life project—setting goals and breaking them into smaller, manageable steps. Support from friends, family, and professional guidance can also make a big difference.[32]

Not everyone gets the chance to choose the ideal job. First jobs are often temporary, a test of one's ability to adapt and grow despite the challenges. However, these initial or 'odd' jobs can offer opportunities to explore new directions and even open the door to unexpected career paths

Mid-Life Crisis

Many people go through a period of inner conflict between the ages of 40 and 60. Some may face physical changes, boredom in their careers or relationships, and feelings of sadness or dissatisfaction.

These emotions often come with negative thoughts about past achievements and a strong desire for change or new challenges.

Common causes include hormonal shifts—such as menopause or andropause—and major life events like children moving out, frequent arguments with a spouse, or ongoing problems at work.

This phase can sometimes lead to anxiety, depression, risky behavior, or unwise life decisions.[33]

Fig. 30: Is this my mid-life crisis?

Managing a mid-life crisis starts with accepting one's limitations, taking time to relax, and recognizing that current emotions can be misleading—often driven by temporary feelings or physical changes beyond our control.

This is a time to show resilience and avoid drastic decisions. Past achievements can offer reassurance and strength for the future. With time, a sense of meaning usually returns, and life—as it was—is appreciated again.[34]

Late-Life Crisis

This difficult period often comes with aging and retirement. Major events—such as losing loved ones or facing health problems—can lead to a loss of direction. Retirement may also bring significant changes to daily routines, and when combined with a sense of no longer being useful, it can affect how people view and use their time.[35]

Late-life crises might cause individuals to feel lost, lonely, or depressed, and to struggle with questions about their identity and life purpose.[36] However, this stage of life can also be an opportunity to think about the future in new ways—by sharing work experience, discovering new hobbies, exploring alternative forms of work, and building a fulfilling life beyond past routines. It also offers the chance to spend more time with loved ones and to become more available to them.

Do We Benefit from Crises?

Crises play an important role in our lives. By bringing us to our knees, they spark a healing process—correcting deficiencies and preparing us to face the next challenge. "A positive resolution of a crisis makes it possible to achieve a new quality in a person's attitude towards themselves and the world, and thus to achieve a higher degree of development of one's personality."[37]

For many, it may be surprising to realize that we are, in a way, programmed: each stage of life serves a purpose and leads to a new challenge. This is marvelous.

We are designed not only to mature physically but also spiritually and psychologically.

The well-known studies of Erik Erikson confirm this. His stages of psychological development reveal a design that leads to personal growth and the achievement of specific goals through conflicts. Erikson defines eight stages, four of which are more relevant to our discussion on crisis and are, for the sake of brevity, compressed and summarized here[38]:

- In our teenage years, we start figuring out who we are and where we belong. This is when we begin forming a sense of identity. The key value here is fidelity—the ability to stay true to ourselves and stand by the choices we make.

- As we move into early adulthood, our focus shifts to building meaningful friendships and romantic relationships. When we navigate this stage well, we gain the capacity for love—deep emotional bonds and a sense of belonging in a wider community.

- By middle adulthood, our energy turns toward contributing—whether at work or within our families. This stage centers on care: finding purpose in helping others grow and leaving a positive mark on the world around us.

- In late adulthood, reflection becomes important. We look back at our lives and try to make sense of it all. If we feel satisfied and at peace with our journey, we gain wisdom —a deeper understanding that comes from lived experience.

Erikson shows that every stage pushes us to grow through challenges. Our personality continues to develop even into old age—this is the innovative contribution of his theory. Light and shadow combine within us to shape individuality: we learn from our mistakes; we strengthen ourselves by overcoming them.

Yet not all life stages follow the rhythm of growth that Erikson outlined. Some experiences overwhelm rather than shape us. Depression, for instance, is not simply another stage in the chart of human development. Those who suffer from it are often pushed beyond the ordinary challenges of life.

Depression

Depression symptoms do not result from developmental crises but from extraordinary circumstances like traumatic life events, social isolation, chronic or extreme situations of stress. It should be treated separately because the foundation of depression is considered to be a complex interaction of biological factors (like brain chemistry imbalances), genetic predisposition, and environmental stressors. No single factor is solely responsible for causing depression.

Depression as a disease is a state of terrible collapse that is much greater than any deterioration produced by the vicissitudes of life. In some cases, the situation can become so overwhelming that individuals might see self-harm as the only way out. These cases are uncommon and need specialized medical attention.

To better understand and recognize the signs of depression, it is important to have some basic knowledge about the illness. This can help us support ourselves and others without overstepping the role of the doctor.

Symptoms

The most common symptoms among those who start suffering from depression are:

The person is not disabled. People in this stage may lack the will to act, as if disengaged from both themselves and the outside world. This inaction can lead to becoming absorbed in a negative mindset and losing interest in the world around them.

Prolonged sadness. There is a prolonged sadness that, even if not very severe, leads to fatigue, low self-esteem, disrupted sleep, indecision, hopelessness, and sometimes personality disorders. This can affect emotional, social, and thinking skills, including concentration and memory, and may impair problem-solving abilities or clear thinking.

Physical disorders. It is common for this emotional state to manifest in certain physical disorders, typically involving digestive issues or headaches. In many cases, the individual struggles to comprehend what is happening to them, which heightens their sense of confusion and anxiety.

Fig. 31: Lost in the shadows of the mind (*Freepik*).

Physiological Foundations

It's all about neurotransmitters. A neurotransmitter is a chemical messenger in the brain that helps carry signals between nerve cells. These messengers play a vital role in regulating mood, memory, movement, and other functions. When neurotransmitters are defective or absent, they can affect the way we think and feel. For example, low levels of certain neurotransmitters—like serotonin—are linked to feelings of sadness or depression.[39]

A person experiencing depression may need medical treatment, depending on the severity of their condition. Antidepressant medications are often prescribed to help restore neurotransmitter balance and improve brain function in individual's depression.

People who begin experiencing symptoms of depression should understand that it's not just a difficult or withdrawn attitude, but a genuine illness they are going through. We can always help by offering empathy, care, and companionship—even when the person's mental state seems unresponsive.

The Burnout Syndrome or Job Burnout

Burnout syndrome is a state of physical, emotional, and mental exhaustion. It is common in today's fast-paced, high-pressure work environments.

The causes are obvious: burnout originates from prolonged work pressure, heavy responsibilities, long working hours, and friction with colleagues and superiors. These factors accumulate over time and leave individuals unable to perform their tasks effectively.

As common as it is, burnout is often disregarded by company policies that continue to demand more and more from employees. Other contributing factors include complications from self-employment, pressure from debt, or the need to increase income for the family.

People suffering from burnout syndrome often fail to recognize that they need help. Those around them—especially supervisors, colleagues, and family—can play a key role in identifying early signs of the condition. Telltale indicators include noticeable personality changes, such as becoming hard, cold, and indifferent toward others, often accompanied by dehumanized reactions.

Other symptoms include emotional stress, mood swings, irritability, and negative attitudes in both work and family environments. Sufferers may withdraw socially, preferring solitude over companionship, and struggle with concentration, task completion, and chronic lateness due to constant exhaustion.

Home remedies include finding a healthier work-life balance, prioritizing sleep and regular exercise, setting aside time for relaxation and meditation to reduce stress, and—when needed—seeking medical advice.

"The best possible remedies for burnout syndromes are controlling stress, letting go of negative thoughts, calming the mind, asking for help in finding solutions, learning to think positively, enhancing management skills, finding inspiration, setting goals at work, considering the pros and cons of quitting the job, and discovering the true purpose in life, can help extinguish burn out and live in the present with happiness."[40]

Life Lessons and Takeaways

I have always supported the idea that knowing what we face strengthens our response. Knowledge gives us always the upper hand. This, I hope, justifies the selection of topics presented in the final chapter of this book.

However, knowledge alone is not enough. Even when we feel self-sufficient, we still realize the importance of finding strength and support in others. At the core of human nature lies the need for companionship. We are social beings: we form communities, cooperate to meet shared needs, and improve our lives through collective effort. Our individuality takes years to mature, shaped not in isolation but through the influence of parents, caregivers, teachers, and the wider environment.

We need company. We need help. We need care. We seek companionship, but we also offer it—and it is in this offering that true maturity is revealed.

Showing genuine care and concern is never easy. Yet the person who strives to correct personal flaws and cultivate character demonstrates progress by developing what might be called a sixth sense: the capacity to care. This marks the summit of authentic character growth.

Such a person remains attentive to those navigating developmental crises—ready to listen, to advise when appropriate, and to walk alongside those they care for through each stage of the struggle.

In this commitment to others, maturity finds its fullest expression.

Conclusion

This book has probably opened the door to challenges we may not have considered before, especially the ongoing task of shaping a character that reflects the subtleties of our personality.

One question that tends to come up is: "Aren't we just turning into robots? Isn't character becoming something we copy rather than something we live?" The fact that we are physically so different—impossibly unique (consider that any adult consists of at least 32 billion cells)—also makes us perceptively, emotionally, and intellectually distinct.

Obviously, character is not limited to the development of five isolated pillars, no matter how essential they may be. It is holistic and defining—it shapes individuals in their unique personal capacities, with each pillar of character contributing a distinct set of values that cannot be equally developed in any two people. On top of that is the way these values interact with personality traits, giving us a formula of complexity and variety.

However, what can we say about their absence? Even when character-values are missing, we remain different. But does this justify a passive attitude—one that, in some ways, offers an easier path? As mentioned at the beginning of this book, character is the energy within. Though we are still different from one another, the absence of most character-values limits our potential.

Reflecting on how people live and work, we observe patterns of behavior that—contrary to what character fosters—render individuals deficient and, in some ways, similar, though again, never identical.

Topics of conversation and opinions tend to be quite similar in most working environments. Opinions about men or women—including lewd jokes and remarks—along with critical views on politics and politicians, and discussions about sports news and events, seem so important that, without them, people often don't know what else to talk about (intellectual character).

Most ethical values are absent from both the public and private lives of those who adopt the most fashionable moral viewpoints of the majority—often with an unspoken fear of expressing differing perspectives (ethical or moral character).

Attitudes toward work truly vary, but they are usually rooted in a desire to do the bare minimum and avoid complications—things that only the boss seems to consider truly important (performance character).

Emotional conflicts arise when people are pulled out of their small, self-centered worlds. This often happens, for example, when they are asked to help beyond their basic obligations—something they see as unacceptable or even disrespectful (emotional literacy).

Lastly, certain manners of conversation—marked by cursing and disrespectful tones—are rapidly spreading across many social levels (though not in every country), making communication increasingly superficial and irrelevant (social character).

It would be unjust to generalize about the absence of developmental values in society. Contrasts are evident in many communities where the pillars of character still hold meaning. However, the examples above highlight the importance of their role: we should live by these values if we want to make our society truly human. We should never stop emphasizing this point.

In the end, the values our society lives by—particularly in the communities where we live and work—depend entirely on the values we choose to live for. Our personal commitment to growth plays a critical role in shaping the communities around us. This likely explains the interest you showed in completing this book.

It is important to emphasize that character is not a passive attitude rooted in expectations about what we will become or what we possess. It is an active disposition that begins, above all, with understanding. The five pillars of character serve as a guide to that understanding. To summarize what was previously outlined:

1. Intellectual Character is perhaps the most important pillar, our foundation and guide in the process of understanding. Without intellectual character, the other four pillars lack grounding.

2. Moral or Ethical Character makes us human. It gives us the ability to respond to every situation with constructive principles, encouraging thoughtful and responsible behavior.

3. Performance Character is a permanent disposition to grow through both favorable and adverse circumstances. It reflects a commitment to benefiting oneself and others.

4. Emotional Literacy is critical for recognizing, recovering from, and managing emotional responses in order to achieve emotional balance.

5. Social or Civic Character integrates us into the community of people who make up the environment we live in—and live for.

By nurturing the five pillars of character, we fortify not only the fabric of society but also the essence of who we are as individuals.

Tex

About the Author

The author–by the nickname of Tex, obtained a Licentiate in Biology with a specialization in Zoology from the State University of Valencia, Spain. He also completed a Certificate in Education at the University of Alicante, which qualified him for teaching positions. Additionally, he holds a Diploma in Affectivity and Sexuality from the University of Navarre in Spain.

In the Philippines he ventured into other fields to add to his humanistic and technical formation finishing a master's in library and information sciences by the University of the Philippines in Diliman, that he completed with a sub specialty in library software and history and the publication of articles in specialized journals together with the printing of the book *History of Books and Libraries in the Philippines, 1521-1900*. He has also published software for library management.

He has occupied management positions in cultural centers, lectured extensively about value education, engaged in school consultancies, mentoring, and counseling. He is an avid cyclist and motorist and has been everywhere North to South in the Philippines.

Other Works by the Author

Tex Hernandez is the author of several thought-provoking books that explore some of life's biggest questions—touching on values like personal growth, relationships, identity, and decision-making. His works are brought together under the engaging umbrella of *The Big-Question Series*, with each title offering a fresh take on challenges we all face.

Am I an Atheist? Science, Atheism, and the Way of Friendship – A thoughtful look at the relationship between science and belief, and how both shape the way we connect with others.

Should I Marry? The Essential Guide to Discernment – A guide to understanding what makes commitment meaningful and how it relates to happiness and lasting success.

Shall I Dress It? Sexuality in Overdrive – An eye-opening examination of the powerful pull of sexuality, including perspectives on addiction and identity.

What Are My Chances? Life Management Explained – A practical and inspiring guide to navigating life's choices and finding a sense of purpose through planning.

Why Character? The Quest That Matters – The newest addition, offering fresh insights into character development through five essential pillars.

All titles in *The Big-Question Series* are available online via Google Play Books and Amazon Kindle.

Notes

[1] The phrase "If you're not growing, you're dying" is often attributed to motivational speaker and author Tony Robbins.

[2] NeuroLaunch Editorial Team, 'PIES Framework,' September 30, 2024 (https://neurolaunch.com/pies-physical-intellectual-emotional-social/?form=MG0AV3).

[3] TTAC Online, 'The Six Pillars of Character (Character Counts!),' 2024 (ttaconline.org).

[4] Curtis Florence, *Five Pillars of Great Character* (North Charleston, SC: CreateSpace Independent Publishing Platform, 2015).

[5] Carlos Beltramo, "Cinco pilares del carácter y apertura a la trascendencia," In M. L. Diez Canseco Briceño (Ed.), *Actas del seminario, Psicología desde una visión cristiana del hombre* (pp. 7–18) (Arequipa, Perú: Universidad Católica San Pablo, 2023) (https://ucsp.edu.pe/actas-seminario-psicologia-desde-vision-cristiana-hombre/).

[6] Jack Maden, 'Socratic Method: What Is It and How Can You Use It?' Philosophy Break, July 2021 (https://philosophybreak.com/articles/socratic-method-what-is-it-how-can-you-use-it/?form=MG0AV3).

[7] Wikipedia, 'Sincerity,' 20 November 2023 (www. Wikipedia. Org).

[8] Conversation with ChatGPT, 'Universal Ethical Laws accepted by the majority of people,' December 16, 2024. The sources are a combination of responses from Christianity, Buddhism, Confucianism, Islam, Bioethics, John Rawls' Theory of Justice, Human Rights declarations, Thomas Hobbes Ethical Philosophy, Aristotle's Virtues and Ethics, Deontology, Utilitarianism, and Legal Systems.

[9] Conversation with ChatGPT, 'Ripley's Believe it or not,' December 28, 2024.

[10] Paul Johnson, *The Quest for God: A Personal Pilgrimage*, Chapter One, 'Why Am I Writing This Book' (New York: HarperCollins, 1996). A thrilling reading that leaves no stone unturned.

[11] Alessandro Bucciol and Marco Piovesan, 'Luck or Cheating? A Field Experiment on Honesty with Children,' November 2008 (https://www.academia.edu/20454899/Luck_or_cheating_A_field_experiment_on_honesty_with_children).

[12] Caroline Bologna, HuffPost, 'Kids Are Not Born Selfish. Here's How to Keep Them That Way,' 29 July 2020 (https://lsa.umich.edu/psych/news-events/all-news/faculty-news/kids-are-not-born-selfish--here-s-how-to-keep-them-that-way-.html).

[13] John Kleinig, 'Loyalty,' Stanford Encyclopedia of Philosophy, March 22, 2022 (https://plato.stanford.edu/entries/loyalty/).

[14] An intelligence quotient (IQ) is a total score derived from a set of standardized tests or subtests designed to assess human intelligence. Scores from intelligence tests are estimates of intelligence. IQ scores are used for educational placement, assessment of intellectual ability, and evaluating job applicants (Wikipedia, 'Intelligence quotient,' December 21, 2024, wikipedia.org).

[15] Alexandre Havard, *From Temperament to Character: On Becoming a Virtuous Leader* (Scepter Publishers, 2021).

[16] The works of Alexandre Havard are essential to anyone who wishes to understand essentials and bring about change.

[17] Constructivism refers to the view that knowledge is actively constructed by individuals rather than passively received from the external world. This is in contrast with positivist or realist approaches, which assume knowledge can be objectively discovered.

[18] National Institute of Mental Health (NIMH), 'Understanding Psychosis' (https://www.nimh.nih.gov/health/publications/understanding-psychosis#part_10942).

[19] NHS (UK National Health Service), 'Causes – Psychosis,' 5 September 2023 (https://www.nhs.uk/mental-health/conditions/psychosis/causes/).

[20] Until 1973, homosexuality was classified as a mental disorder in the Diagnostic and Statistical Manual of Mental Disorders (DSM) by the American Psychiatric Association (APA). This classification was challenged by activists and researchers, notably Dr. Evelyn Hooker, whose 1950s studies showed no difference in mental health between homosexual and heterosexual men. In 1973, the APA voted to remove homosexuality from the DSM though a residual category called "sexual orientation disturbance" remained until 1987 (see Neel Burton, 'When Homosexuality Stopped Being a Mental Disorder,' *Psychology Today*, June 2024, psychologytoday.com). Well-known psychiatrists like Dr. Irving Bieber and Dr. Charles Socarides have challenged this decision. The later founded the National Association for Research and Therapy of Homosexuality (NARTH) and published extensively on the controversy (see, *Homosexuality: A Freedom Too Far*, 1995), promoting reparative therapy. He has been widely criticized and marginalized for his views.

[21] Socialigence, 'Social Intelligence in Research,' 2015 (https://www.socialigence.net/blog/social-intelligence-in-research/?form=MG0AV3).

[22] Elena L. Grigorenko, 'Intelligence, Social,' in Encyclopedia.com, 2019 (https://www.encyclopedia.com/social-sciences/applied-and-social-sciences-magazines/intelligence-social?form=MG0AV3).

[23] Bastian Herre and others, 'Marriages and Divorces,' *Our World in Data*, February 2025 (https://ourworldindata.org/marriages-and-divorces).

[24] Christy Bieber, 'Reveling Divorce Statistics in 2025,' *Forbes*, November 20, 2024' (https://www.forbes.com/advisor/legal/divorce/divorce-statistics/).

[25] Publicmitra, 'Global Divorce Rates: A Comprehensive Analysis of Marriage Dissolution Worldwide in 2024-2025' (https://publicmitra.com/support-legally/global-divorce-rates-a-

comprehensive-analysis-of-marriage-dissolution-worldwide-in-2024-2025/).

[26] Karl Albrecht, around 2009, elaborated the five major dimensions of social intelligence as situational radar, presence/bearing, authenticity, clarity and empathy which I have modified slightly for the purpose of clarity. You can read all about it in Socialigence's article cited above ('Social Intelligence in Research').

[27] 'Model of Communication,' Wikipedia, November 3, 2024 (https://en.wikipedia.org/)

[28] This summary is but a simplification of the better-known linear communication models which are (1) the Aristotle's model, (2) the Lasswell's model, (3) the Shannon-Weaver model, and (4) the Berlo's S-M-C-R model. You will find a full description of what each model represents in Jelena Fisic, '8 Communication Models: Understanding What They Are and How They Work,' 29 September 2023 (https://pumble.com/learn/communication/communication-models/).

[29] David A. Carbonell, *The Worry Free Trick* (Oakland, California: New Harbinger Publications, 2016). A recommended reading for all.

[30] Sagari Gongala, '11 Common Problems of Adolescence and their Solutions,' January 10, 2025 (https://www.momjunction.com/articles/problems-of-adolescence_00381378/?form=MG0AV3).

[31] Madeline Miles, '4 Ways to Overcome Your Quarter-Life Crisis (and redefining success),' May 12, 2022 (https://www.betterup.com/blog/quarter-life-crisis?form=MG0AV3).

[32] Charlie Health Editorial Team, 'Signs You're Having a Quarter-Life Crisis (and what to do),' August 15, 2024 (https://www.charliehealth.com/post/quarter-life-crisis?form=MG0AV3).

[33] MindHelp, 'Midlife Crisis,' 2025 (https://mind.help/topic/midlife-crisis/?form=MG0AV3).

[34] Sheldon Reid, 'Midlife Crisis, Signs, Causes, and Coping Tips,' 2025 (https://www.helpguide.org/aging/healthy-aging/midlife-crisis?form=MG0AV3).

[35] Alicia Ines Arbaje, 'Coping with a Late-Life Crisis,' 2025 (https://www.hopkinsmedicine.org/health/caregiving/caregiver-guides/coping-with-a-later-life-crisis?form=MG0AV3).

[36] Richard J. Leider and David A. Shapiro, 'Are You Having a Late-Life Crisis?' July 16, 2021 (https://www.nextavenue.org/late-life-crisis/?form=MG0AV3).

[37] Ewa Krokosz, 'The Role of Crises in Human Development,' *Journal of Security and Sustainability Issues*, Vol. 13, 2023, pp. 2 & 3 (https://doi.org/10.47459/jssi.2023.13.22).

[38] If you are interested in the complete 'Erikson's stages of psychosocial development,' let me refer to you to the article published on Wikipedia, updated in November 2025 (https://en.wikipedia.org/wiki/Erikson%27s_stages_of_psychosocial_development). You can also read the article of Kendra Cherry, updated November 2025 in *Verywellmind* (https://verywellmind.com/erik-eriksons-stages-of-psychosocial-develolment).

[39] Conversation with ChatGPT, 'Explain in common terms what is a neurotransmitter,' February 3, 2025.

[40] Lanchasak Akkayagorn, 'Burnout Syndromes,' *MedPark Hospital*, May 31, 2023 (https://www.medparkhospital.com/en-US/lifestyles/burnout-syndrome)

Made in the USA
Coppell, TX
28 February 2026

72589566R00075